40p

D1585214

By the same author

Focus on the Falkland Islands

Margaret Stewart Taylor

THE TRAVEL BOOK CLUB
121 Charing Cross Road, London WC2

PRINTED IN GREAT BRITAIN BY
CLARKE, DOBLE & BRENDON LTD,
PLYMOUTH

Contents

Illustrations

*With the exception of the first photograph, provided
by Mr. Willie May, all pictures were taken by the
author*

I

Islands of Solitude

WHEN Queen Victoria died the British Empire, "on which the sun never set", was at the height of its glory. Maps of the world were sprinkled with red blobs, large and small, each blob denoting territory that was a British colony; but since 1901 the spirit of acquisition has gradually been replaced by the spirit of dispossession—at least as regards Britain. As a result Victoria's great-great-grandchild, Queen Elizabeth II, has barely half a dozen colonies left under her suzerainty. One of these survivors is a cluster of islands in the South Atlantic Ocean called the Falkland Islands.

Eight thousand, one hundred and three miles separate them from the mother country, and although they lie within similar latitudes to our counties of Lancashire and Yorkshire, yet biting winds from the Cape Horn region and icy currents flowing from Antarctic seas make the climate far more severe. The average temperature on the Falklands is consistently well below that experienced in such places as Liverpool and Hull.

There were no human beings on the islands when Captain Strong made the first known landing in 1690. They had been sighted ninety-eight years earlier by another English mariner, John Davis, and today his ship, *Desire*, features in the coat-of-arms and has inspired the motto, "Desire the Right." The next landing was made by a Frenchman, Gouin de Beauchêne, and by 1766 there were two small settlements, one French and one British; but in that year France withdrew from hers in response to pressure from Spain, and Spain took it over. This is the basis of one of Argentina's claims to have the Falklands under her rule.

The group consists of two large islands and about 200 small

ones, the entire mass of land, to quote from the Foreign and Commonwealth Office's biennial reports, being "comparable in area with Northern Ireland but spread over a much greater extent". The Falklands were designated a Crown Colony in 1892, but governors who represented the reigning monarch were sent there from 1842 onwards, ten years after Britain decided to colonize the islands in earnest. At the time of the 1962 census the population numbered 2,172. Ninety-eight per cent at least were of British stock, the remainder being immigrants—usually temporary—from Uruguay and Chile. The only other foreigners in 1969 that I heard lived there were a woman from the United States and a Polish doctor from Antarctica, but whether or not he had been granted British citizenship I do not know.

Right of possession has been disputed between Argentina and Britain for 140 years, the wrangle only receiving world attention in 1965 when Argentina brought her claims before the United Nations. Even then most British people remained unaware of this Crown Colony's existence or were vague about its geographical position, confusing the Falklands with the Shetlands or the West Indies. Then, for a short time in November 1968, the islands became front page news. Lord Chalfont, Minister of State Foreign and Commonwealth Office was sent on a mission that was said to be for discussions about the future with governor and legislative council, but some newspapers hinted darkly that he was to announce a hand-over of the territory to Argentina, who, in return, would grant Britain meat concessions. This was promptly denied and Parliament was assured that the British government only planned to arrange talks with Argentina in response to a request from the United Nations, and there would be no transfer of sovereignty without consent of the Falkland Islanders. The crisis subsided and the colony's future ceased to occupy the thoughts of men and women in Britain who lived 8,000 miles away, in fact at the other end of the world.

When I visited the Falklands a year later, talks had not started, but it was anticipated they might begin at any time and people were apprehensive about the effect on their future. On 29th October, in an official address to the Legislative Council, the Governor referred "to the possibility, politics apart, of the opening up of communications with Argentina". Now there has been a Berlin Wall between the two countries for more than twenty years, and to go to Argentina with a Falkland Islands passport, so I was told, was to risk police questionings, even risk of internment. It is no wonder such strong anti-Argentine feeling exists among Falklanders.

The Governor announced over the local radio that the two governments, British and Argentine, would be holding talks early in 1970, but "representatives from the Falkland Islands have been invited to participate". This broadcast sparked off such remarks as, "Our standard of living will go down under the Argies." "They will make us speak Spanish and we don't know the language." "I shall emigrate to New Zealand." "I'm sick to death of this argy-bargy with the Argies. Why must Britain bother with talks? Why can't we be left alone?"

There was a rumour that Argentina was offering to build a badly-needed air strip on the Falklands, and that the British Government would ignore local opposition and accept the offer. Someone said to me, "Then we shall see the two flags flying side by side for about a year. After that the Argies will haul down the Union Jack, and we shall become the Malvinas." Las Isles Malvinas is what Argentina calls the Falklands.

She bases her claim to them on four points: the right to inherit a former Spanish Empire possession; the iniquity of colonization; the geological relationship between the Falklands and the South American mainland; and that they lie off the coast of Patagonia, a region of Argentina.

Nobody denies the fourth statement. Stanley, the only town and full port on the Falklands, is 300 miles from the Argentine port of Gallegos, so sailings between the two would be a great convenience; but at present there are none because of the dispute. Communications with the outer world are made by the Falklands with Argentina's two neighbours, Uruguay and Chile. The nearest Chilean port is Punta Arenas at the extreme south of Latin America, and only occasional ships sail there from Stanley. Regular traffic goes to the Uruguay port of Montevideo, a distance of 1,000 miles. Once a month the mailship, *Darwin*, leaves the Falklands for 'Monte' on what is a three to four day voyage but may be longer in bad weather, and when I was in Stanley the *Darwin* took six days on one return trip because of

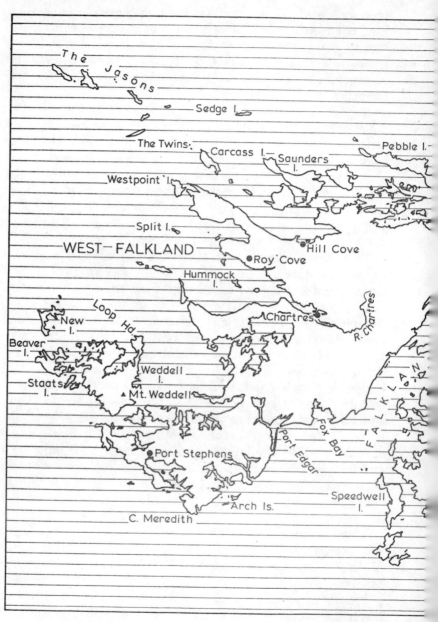

SOUTH
AMERICA

ATLANTIC
OCEAN

FALKLAND
ISLANDS
Beauchêne
I.

·Eddystone Rock

Douglas
Settlement●
Port San
Carlos

Salvador
Salvador
Waters

Rincon Grande

Johnson's
Hr.

Volun-
teer
Pt.

San Carlos

Teal
Inlet

Port
Louis

Berkeley
Sound

Kidney
I.

Green
Patch

Port
William

'ort
Ioward

R Malo

Stanley

Fitzroy
Settlement●

Sapper
Hill

Darwin
Goose Green

LAFONIA

EAST‑FALKLAND

Lively I.

Trieste I.

Motley I.

Bleaker I.

Sea Lion Is.

0   Miles   20

severe gales. A port 700 miles nearer would certainly benefit the islands. However, does proximity justify a nation's claim to outside territory? On such grounds, France could demand the Channel Islands from Britain. Italy could demand Corsica from France.

Turning to the geological aspect, experts say the Falklands are structurally allied with Africa not South America. Far back in the aeons of time the two continents may have been joined by a land mass—called Gondwanaland by geologists—and the theory is that this was eventually submerged by the Atlantic Ocean. If that occurred some fragments of the African end, a portion of the Karro, may have drifted westward and became the Falkland Islands. In the *Geological Magazine* for 1952, R. J. Adie propounds this theory and asserts them to be "one of the far-travelled masses", bearing "no stratigraphical or structural relation to Patagonia, but to South Africa".

Then Argentina argues that the Falklanders are not natives, but British colonists, so their presence contravenes that section of the Monroe Doctrine which condemns colonialism. It could be said that any settlers sent to the islands by Argentina would also be colonials. There were no natives when the islands were discovered, and at least 80 per cent of the present inhabitants were born there.

The historical claim is very involved. Both Britain and France established small settlements in the latter half of the eighteenth century, but the French one at Port Louis on East Falkland preceded the British one—Port Egmont, on what is now Saunders Island—by a year. Spain heard the French were occupying territory that she considered was part of her New World Empire and demanded their withdrawal. In 1766 France yielded Port Louis to the Spaniards, who changed the name to Puerta de la Soledad. They called the East Falkland, Isla Nuestra Señora de la Soledad, Island of Our Lady of Solitude.

It seems to have been a couple of years before they realized that Britain had a settlement on an island adjacent to the West Falkland, and when they did protests and skirmishes ensued. Later the Spanish government made threats to the British government. There were attempts at negotiations that broke down, but in 1774, mainly due to economy cuts, Britain withdrew her garrison from Port Egmont, thus leaving Spain in sole possession until thirty-six years later when the latter's South American colonies revolted and she lost her New World Empire. The United Provinces of La Plata came into existence, with government headquarters in Buenos Aires, and this new state unsuccessfully tried to found a fresh colony at Puerta de la Soledad. Spain had had a penal settlement on the islands and now the United Provinces started one at San Carlos.

In 1833 Britain reasserted her rights over the Falklands, declaring she could lawfully do so since her settlement preceded Spain's. Besides, though France did transfer her settlement—the first—to that country, yet Spain had not ceded it to the United Provinces of La Plata, now the Argentine Republic. Argentina says the Falklands were part of the former Spanish Empire, and therefore now belong to her. *"Las Malvinas son nuestras"* is taught to every child, and this belief is so ingrained in the nation that the cry *"nuestras"* or "ours" echoes from Buenos Aires to Ushuaia.

I had not been long in Stanley when I was told about the Argentine 'token invasion' of September 1966. There is a society called Condor, which is dedicated to the cause of 'getting back' the Falklands, and twenty of its members hi-jacked a plane travelling from Buenos Aires to Gallegos with twenty-six other passengers on board. Under the mistaken impression that there was an airport on the Falkland Islands, they compelled the pilot to change course, and Falklanders were amazed to see this air-liner overhead, apparently seeking a landing ground.

"We saw a four-engined plane flying over Stanley from west to east. There was no cloud and the aircraft was fairly low. I thought at the time 'I hope they know there are some new masts up to the west of the town because I do not think the red lights on their tops are alight yet.' Anyway, the plane turned round and came along Ross Road with the wheels down, skimmed the Cathedral, and it was obvious that a landing was going to be attempted—with such a large craft this did not seem possible."

The plane crashed on the Stanley racecourse. I met some people living in Ross Road West where backs of the houses faced the course. They rushed out with offers of assistance, assuming it to be in distress and maybe passengers injured. A few snatched up cameras to take pictures of this phenomenal occurrence. Nothing like it had ever happened before. Crowds on foot and others in Land-Rovers converged on the scene. One of the first to arrive was a police sergeant, and to everyone's astonishment he was pushed into the plane at gun point, while one of the visitors planted an Argentine flag in the ground. Then it dawned on the Falklanders that this was no accidental air crash but a demonstration with aggressive intentions.

There were only seven policemen, and one had been taken prisoner, but the remainder cordoned off the area. Neither side could understand the other. It surprised the Condor group that no-one spoke Spanish, for they imagined that the islands were full of Argentinians waiting liberation from British rule. At last a Spanish-speaking person was found to act as interpreter, and the Condor leader explained they had come from 22 million countrymen to end the English invasion of the Malvinas 132 years ago. He could not understand why the watching crowd did not proclaim their joy when the interpreter shouted the message in English. He and his companions not only expected the Falkland Islanders to cry, "This is the day of deliverance!" but also to escort the liberators through the streets of Stanley in triumph. Meanwhile they stood with their firearms around the wrecked plane and prevented the other passengers from leaving it.

These passengers whose journey had been interrupted by the hi-jacking included the Argentinian governor of Tierra del Fuego, another Minister of State bound for Santa Cruz, and a well-known boxer who had a professional engagement at Gallegos. Eventually the Condor group allowed them to leave and to accept offers of hospitality in Stanley. They were amazed at the comfort and high standard of living, having believed that Falklanders lived in shacks and hovels like the poorest folk in Argentina. It was also a surprise that only English was spoken and that there was no airport.

The Condor group did not surrender for another twenty-four hours. Then they gave up their arms and were marched away under guard. The acting governor had already got in touch with London by telephone. He was told that a battleship, H.M.S. *Puma*, was being sent direct from Simonstown. Contact was made as well with Buenos Aires, and Argentina promised to send a naval vessel to collect her citizens. It would wait outside territorial waters at a pre-arranged spot where they could be brought by a British ship. This did not prove to be so easy to carry out as was expected. The *Philomel* left Stanley with the Condor group defiantly singing Argentinian patriotic songs. They were very angry, as well as disillusioned over the failure of their liberation mission, and could not have been more eager to leave than were the other passengers who had been victims of the hi-jacking. The pilot and assistants stayed behind trying to extricate the damaged plane from the boggy land where it was stuck, managed to get it airborne at last, and flew back to Buenos Aires. As for the *Philomel* passengers, once outside Stanley harbour the sea was very choppy and seasickness soon stopped the young Condors from singing. Most of them turned out to be poor sailors. *Philomel* reached the Argentinian ship, but it was too rough for her to get alongside so she was obliged to return to Stanley with her disconsolate passengers and wait until next day, hoping the weather would improve. The second journey was successful. The Condor enthusiasts revived enough to recommence singing as they boarded their country's vessel, but as the Argentinian government had disclaimed responsibility for the escapade there was not the welcome they expected. Instead, sailors lined up on deck received them in silence, and they were at once placed under arrest.

Memories of this incident made the Falkland Islands authorities nervous lest there be a repetition during Lord Chalfont's visit four years later, and the racecourse was blocked, making it impossible for any aircraft to land. The precautions turned out to be necessary. An Argentine private plane, named 'Cronica', came on a second mission. It was privately owned by a wealthy member of the Condors, and others from the society accompanied him. Finding the racecourse was useless they were forced to come down on moorland near Eliza Cove, just outside Stanley, and, as before, crowds flocked to the spot. But this time the Condors were more knowledgeable about the Falklands. They realized the Islanders were of British, not South American origin, and that they only spoke English, so leaflets in that language had been prepared for general distribution as well as St. Christopher medals.

The leaflet began, "We don't come as aggressors, but as Argentine citizens to meet again with our country and with

B

men of this country which are our brothers." The English was often stilted and had grammatical errors. It was stated that the islands would be known as the Malvinas when they were returned to Argentina, and that Stanley would be renamed Port Rivero. All people born on the Malvinas would be granted "rights [and] benefits" of the Argentine republic, which promised "to declare Private Property to all the Malvina homes and to Adjudge to all the Natives their farms or their homes". The use of the word 'native' was a blunder, for no appellation is considered more insulting. You can call the Falkland Islander an islander or a Kelper, but never a native.

This second plane venture ended as ignominiously as the first, except that instead of flying back to Buenos Aires, the 'Cronica' was too badly damaged and had to be taken to pieces and the parts sent by ship to Montevideo. From the Uruguayan port they went to Argentina.

Both incidents have made people on the Falklands nervous about unidentified aircraft, and should one be sighted people rush into gardens and streets, looking upwards with apprehension. This happened during my visit, and agitation only ceased when an announcement was made over the local radio to explain that the strange plane belonged to the United States and was on a trial flight from Antarctica. Again, an aeroplane was heard one evening after supper and, as the two local Beavers do not normally fly late, my host and hostess were very alarmed, but on going outside Willie May saw it was a Beaver. "Then it has gone for a hospital case," he said. Later, over the radio, we heard a man had been fetched from West Falkland as he urgently needed to be admitted to hospital.

My friends in Britain were as surprised as those first Condor 'invaders' when I said I could not fly from London to the Falklands because the islands had not got an external air service. Even if one flew to Montevideo in South America, then one had to cross the sea by boat. For years construction of an air-strip on the Cape Pembroke peninsula near Stanley has been talked about, but nothing is done because the Falkland Islands government says it cannot afford the money. The latest estimate of the cost for main runway and essential equipment is £265,000, while a subsidiary runway would cost an additional £70,000.

Two single-engined Beaver floatplanes provide a service

between the islands, but they are not capable of long-distance flights. With their floats they take off and come down on water. Each one carries up to six passengers, plus mail and a very small amount of freight. Usually they fly once or twice daily, as required, with an occasional emergency flight, but take-off is impossible from rough water so the service is often interrupted. I met a couple in Stanley who had been staying at Fox Bay West on the West Falkland island—a distance of 95 miles as the crow flies—and their return was delayed for six days because of flights cancelled through bad weather. But with all the disadvantages the air service is a wonderful boon to people living on sheep farms and has broken down some of the isolation that has to be endured on those settlements. Local weather reports are given each morning by radio telephone.

"This is Agnes Davies speaking from New Island. I am afraid it is very overcast here and we are expecting rain." Then from another part of the islands comes, "Carol Miller speaking. We've got a nice bright morning at Port San Carlos." Then would follow messages from the Stanley operator. "Is this Keppel Island? Edith speaking. Hullo, Clifford! Yes, Ian is going to Saunders and Keppel today. He hasn't got a radio on the second Beaver so he'll fly round for you to signal where he is to come down. Hullo, Carcass Island, here is a birthday greeting from. . . ."

I found it fascinating to listen to the radio telephone, spoken of as the R.T., and hear Edith's daily chats.

The internal air service was introduced in 1959, and before that one could only travel round the islands by sea, or overland on horseback. Eleven years later sea is the only way one can get to the outer world, by boat not plane. Apart from naval vessels bringing V.I.P.s, as well as ships belonging to British Antarctic Survey that may take their personnel to Antarctica or to Punto Arenas, there are only two ships carrying ordinary passengers, such as I was. R.M.S. *Darwin*, tonnage 1,792, with accommodation for forty passengers, sails once a month from Stanley to Montevideo, then back again to Stanley. She also makes trips delivering freight and collecting wool clip from sheep-farm settlements scattered around the Falklands. She belongs to the Falkland Islands Trading Company, who say she is run at a heavy loss. However, without this vessel the company could not carry on much of their trade, nor transport personnel, so this deficiency is presumably compensated in other ways. The company also charters a Danish cargo ship, the A.E.S., that makes four trips per annum direct from London to Stanley, and vice versa. Besides conveying freight and carrying up to fifteen passengers, her chief purpose is to take wool clip—sheep farming being the Falklands' only industry and wool their sole export—from Stanley to London, where it is sold at the Spitalfield auctions, being renowned for its soft quality. When I left in January 1970, I travelled on the A.E.S., and she had 1,000 tons of wool clip on board.

The voyage took thirty-one days. It is quicker, but far more expensive, to sail by Darwin to Montevideo, then continue the journey by Blue Star or some other liner, or by S.A.S. airliner. The latter only takes thirty-six hours from Uruguay to Britain, but first one spends a minimum of three and a half days getting to Montevideo from Stanley. An interval of twenty-four hours, or longer, is allowed between connections, and I was told that should the Darwin be delayed by severe weather, then a Blue Star liner would wait for twelve hours, but no more, for passengers coming from the Falklands, and an airliner up to six hours. Of course if you do miss the connection you may have to wait some time in Uruguay for the next ship or plane to Britain, and though, going by air from South America, one can hope to reach London within a week of leaving Stanley, that is the minimum time. Usually the journey takes longer.

This shows how unbelievably isolated are the Falkland Islands. The monthly Darwin, with forty passengers, and the quarterly A.E.S. with fifteen are the only means of arriving and getting away—except for important visitors, urgently-needed British Antarctic Survey personnel, and men bound for the Antarctic bases. During my stay, an ex-governor of Gibraltar, on a private visit, was brought to Stanley by the naval vessel, H.M.S. Endurance. Then I met a girl secretary from the British Antarctic Survey (B.A.S.) Stanley office, and because her services were required in a hurry she was flown from London to Punta Arenas, then came the remaining 400 miles by sea in a B.A.S. ship. This organization has four—R.R.S. John Biscoe, R.R.S. Shackleton, M.V. Kista Dam, and M.V. Perla Dan, all operating between Stanley, South Georgia, Chile and Antarctic bases.

Apart from the exceptions mentioned, I calculate that only 540 people can leave the Falklands in a single year, and the same number arrive. At first sight this seems adequate shipping accommodation for a 2,000 population, but the large number of folk going on leave to Britain, or returning after expiration of contract, makes for congestion from February to July going north, and from August to November coming south. I booked my return passage in the April A.E.S., then changed it to the January boat, my place being filled immediately from the waiting list. The *Darwin* was booked solid from January 1970 until the following August, also the June A.E.S., so I knew if anything like sudden illness prevented me from sailing mid-January and I lost my passage, I should be a prisoner on the Falklands until September. Of course if I were desperately ill—and it would have to be a serious matter—then the Medical Officer of Health could send me to the British hospital in Montevideo, and a few berths on the *Darwin* are always kept in reserve until immediately before sailing time for such emergencies.

Slowness of transport also affects mail, and, as regards surface mail, this takes as long as it did eighty years ago, that is a month or more, to come from Britain. In the Stanley Museum I found a postal notice giving dates, and a letter posted in London by 18th January would arrive at Stanley on 16th February. This was in the year 1892. The year 1970 is no different, unless one sends mail by air when it will only take a week. As for newspapers, I left Stanley on 15th January, and the latest British one I had seen was for the previous mid-November. Few places in the world are now so isolated.

Of the 2,000 or so people on the Falklands, one half lives in Stanley and the remainder is scattered over the 'Camp'. 'Camp' derived from the Spanish word *campo*, meaning country or countryside—covers everywhere else but Stanley, and throughout the Camp are thirty or more farms, sheep farming being the only industry on the islands. Each one is situated on the coast of East or West Falkland, or on a small island, thus enabling wool to be sent away and stores obtained by sea. Except in Stanley, no roads have been built on the Falklands, and it seems unlikely they ever will be. Like an airport, the stumbling block is the high cost, while it can always be argued that the Camp has managed for well over 100 years without roads and therefore can continue to do so. Their construction would be difficult and expensive owing to the numerous peat bogs, impossible to avoid, and over which supporting 'mattresses' of brushwood would be required, and they would have to be deep and sufficiently strong to take the weight of heavy vehicles. Six hundred miles of road would be needed, and the cost would be twice the usual amount per mile and annual maintenance very heavy. Of course the advantages would be enormous. Apart from transport of goods, the education of Camp children could be greatly improved and doctors could get to sick patients more quickly. Roads would also make Camp life more attractive. At present every settlement is cut off from the others. I asked an Australian-born wife if loneliness on a Falkland sheep farm was as bad as in the Australian outback? "Far worse," was her reply. "Distances here are small by comparison, but in Australia we had roads. You can easily drive to a farm 100 miles away, but in the Camp here it is almost impossible to get to one 10 miles distant. You start in a Land-Rover to follow a rough trail but you are soon stuck in a peat bog and it may take an hour to dig yourself out."

When Charles Darwin the naturalist visited the Falklands in 1834, he met gauchos from South America in what is now the Camp, and they took him to see some of the wild cattle. At first British colonists favoured cattle farming, but they soon changed to sheep. The Falkland Islands Trading Company started with a stock of thirty sheep in 1851, and, twenty years later, this had increased to 48,000. Today, on company and other farms, the total number of sheep on the islands is between 600,000 and 700,000, while annual production of wool is about £4¾ million. A small quantity of skins and hides is exported in addition to wool clip, but the mutton is either consumed locally or thrown away. It is through wool that the Falklands have prospered, and while this commodity sells their prosperity will continue.

Turning to Argentina's desire to re-possess the islands, this springs from sentiment and a sense of injury. She knows the territory would be no economic asset to her. Her farmers do not need additional land for sheep or cattle while it would be impossible to grow grain in the Falklands climate. It is thought that Argentina would utilize the islands for a penal settlement, as she twice did in the past. In fact Britain once thought of doing the same. I came across a curious document in the British Museum, printed either in 1841 or 1842, and called *Reasons for the formation of a convict establishment at Falkland Islands.* It set forth points in favour of the scheme. First, there was no native population to be debased by convicts or to shelter run-aways. The islands were a long way from the South American mainland. There were no forests or woods to serve as places of concealment. Finally, convicts could be employed on construction work that was badly needed in a new colony.

"No forests or woods", for the Falklands are devoid of trees and bushes, except in a few places where they have been carefully cultivated and tended. The most noted and extensive of these efforts is the 'forest' at Hill Cove on West Falkland. Nearly fifty years ago a Mr. Robert Blake planted Austrian pines, Antarctic beech, and types of laurel and barbery. For the first six years their survival was doubtful, but they became established, though even now the force of the wind may kill new shoots that rise above the level of shelter made by existing trees.

A treeless landscape is apt to invoke adjectives like 'harsh' and 'ungenial', but the vast expanse of undulating land and rounded hills has its own spectacular charm. None of the hills are really mountains and only three—Usborne (pronounced Osborne), Adam and Wickham—reach a height of 2,000 feet. Slopes and lowlands are covered with coarse grasses, great patches of diddle dee (a kind of heather) and other heaths, outcrops of quartz rock and peat bogs, each of these marked by its colour of green, dark purple, white or blackish-brown, as the case may be. The Falklands have none of the brilliant lush colour of tropical lands, nor the majestic grandeur of islands further south on the fringe of Antarctica. No icebergs drift past the coast, but there are beaches of silvery sand glistening like snow from a distance. Sometimes the sea is deep azure, another day pale blue, and yet again it may vary from emerald green to leaden grey. There is great beauty in the Falkland scenery and the islands have a magnetism drawing back many a Kelper who has left them for the outer world. And when the wind drops, which it does now and then, there is an extraordinary quiet, a tranquility that gives one a deep inner peace and makes the visitor forget the turbulence, the sickness and the rat-race of modern civilization.

The Falkland Islands are a paradise for naturalists, especially ornithologists. I am only an amateur bird-watcher, but I had the thrill of getting so close to species I had never before seen that the binoculars I had brought were quite unnecessary. Birds and marine mammals are so unafraid of man that they will let human beings approach them without any concern. Marine mammals coming to the islands are the southern sea lion, the fur seal, the elephant seal, the leopard seal, while not leaving the sea are porpoises and dolphins. Birds include five kinds of penguin, gulls, skuas, oyster-catchers, ducks, geese and many others. Fortunately the government is alive to the need for proper conservation and already has twelve wild bird and animal sanctuaries. A naturalist, Ian Strange, who lives in Stanley, is very active in this work, declaring that the islands "contain a particularly interesting assemblage of animals and plants of equal interest to those found in other parts of the world".

To quote him further, "Of particular importance is the fact that there has been relatively little interference by man's activities. Many parts, especially the offshore islands, are still largely unspoiled and as such are extremely valuable as 'reference areas' where scientific and ecologic studies can be pursued."

Evidence of the Falklands' increasing attraction for naturalists is shown by their inclusion in itineraries of Lindblad cruises that cater for people wishing to be introduced to wild life. In January 1970 two points of call on the Falklands were West Point Island, nesting ground of the black-browed albatross known locally as the mollymauk; and Carcass Island, haunt of the elephant seal. This is the type of tourist industry that the Falkland Islands government would like to see expand.

But apart from cruise ships, visitors to the Falklands come to take jobs or see relations and friends; there are also men waiting to go to Antarctica and there is the occasional ornithologist. I prefer to call myself a traveller not a tourist, a distinction made by an acquaintance who ran a hotel in the Seychelles. According to him, the tourist grumbled if things went wrong but the traveller took it in his stride. This was the spirit in which I went to the Falklands. I had some surprises though. I had not been long in Stanley before I was amazed to discover that a lone female globe-trotter was considered very extraordinary. Wisely or unwisely, I was quite frank about my purpose in coming, namely to see the islands, study the way of life and write a book about my experiences, but it alienated some Stanley folk, and they were not all Kelpers. If people are suspicious of an author they are uncomfortable in his or her presence. That intrepid Victorian, Mary Kingsley, found it necessary to give a reason, other than enjoyment of scenery, for travelling alone in the wilds of Africa. She pretended to be a trader, or said that she was searching for her errant husband, although he did not exist. On the Falklands I could not have got away with either of those explanations, so it was probably better to have told the truth.

2

Getting to the Falklands

IT was rather a mix-up to be boarding a Danish cargo vessel whose destination was a set of islands owned by Britain and claimed by Argentina. This is what I did on 8th September 1969. A friend from the island of St. Helena was in England and planned to come and see me off, but was unable to do so because the sailing date was changed at the last minute. That is one of the inconveniences of travelling by cargo boat. It is the freight, not the passenger, which is important, so time of departure alters according to speed of loading, as well as other factors.

For more than a year I had been waiting to make this voyage —that is since I first made plans to visit the Falkland Islands. In June 1968, at a cocktail party in Cardiff, I talked to Dr. John, then Director of the National Museum of Wales, about my recent visit to St. Helena, the South Atlantic island where Napoleon Bonaparte was exiled and died. I happened to say I should like to visit another British Crown Colony and Dr. John suggested the Falklands. He had been there in the nineteen-thirties when he was engaged on scientific work in the Antarctic. I went to London shortly after this and called at the offices of the Falkland Islands Trading Company to enquire about ships. The secretary gave me details, warning me it was essential to book outward and return passages in plenty of time as accommodation was limited. I made reservations straightway. Then I went to the British Museum to read all I could find about the islands.

Later on I also got information from people who had been there, including the wife of a former sheep farmer and a former rector of Stanley. I wrote to the Colonial Secretary in the Falklands and, after a two-months interval, I received a helpful reply and a suggestion that I communicate with a Mrs. Gipps, now living in Essex, but who had been out there for several months. It was some time before Mrs. Gipps replied to my letter, but when she did she gave me useful advice about being prepared for the fierce wind, the kind of clothes needed, and so on. However one passage puzzled me.

"I am sorry that I have not replied to your letter earlier. You posed a number of problems which I was unable to answer immediately and my husband had to get in touch with his organization in Stanley." I could not fathom the need for this direct contact, neither had I any idea what was Mr. Gipps' organization. The mystery was not solved till I actually reached the Falklands.

I had already booked at the Ship Hotel in Stanley, the only hotel that took visitors, according to information given in the official biennial report published by Her Majesty's Stationery Office. It interested me to discover that the musical-comedy actress, Ellaline Terriss, later Lady Seymour Hicks, was born there in 1871. Her father went to become partner of a sheep farm with a certain Captain Pack, but only stayed a couple of years, so Ellaline Terriss could not remember anything about the Falklands. I was disappointed over this when I read her autobiography, *Just a Little Bit of String*. However, she said a tablet had been put over the 'Ship's' front door, "In this house the great actress Ellaline Terriss was born." It was not there when I got to Stanley and had apparently been missing for many, many years.

After making so many preparations, it was very exciting to be in a taxi, with five suitcases, and know I was being driven to the Surrey Commercial Docks where the A.E.S., the cargo ship taking me to the Falkland Islands, was berthed. It was so thrilling to be starting on this long-awaited voyage that I could not feel sad at saying good-bye for many months to London's grand buildings and busy streets, to traffic jams, and above all to trees.

The dock quay was crowded with vans and lorries from which goods were being unloaded prior to being hoisted on the ship. A huge bundle of telegraph poles was poised in mid-air. In fact my taximan had difficulty in manœuvring into a space beside a colossal packing case labelled "Rincon Grande, East Falkland". I got out and paid him. Then a pale-faced burly man came down a gangway and announced that he was the chief steward but it was no use telling me his proper name because English people found it so difficult to pronounce Danish and therefore I must call him Kelly. Looking at my luggage he bawled "Al-ann!" and a blond young man came running to help. Between the two my luggage was carried to my cabin— a single one with private shower and toilet.

I was very curious about my fellow-passengers, wondering whether they would all be Falkland Islanders returning home, and if not why they were making the voyage.

"We are full, choc-a-block full," Kelly told me. "Now the lady in the next cabin, she is Mrs. Bonner and she was with us when we came from Stanley last January. She was coming to England to visit her son. And on the way here she had her seventieth birthday, so when I knew this I made her a special iced cake and we had a little celebration. Now come up to the lounge and you will meet her. The Emigration and Customs people will be along soon and they will want to see everyone in the lounge, and documents, so bring your passport."

I and the fourteen other passengers—ten men and four women—sat there awkwardly, trying to be sociable while we waited for the officials but furtively eyeing one another. We were like a group of actors assembled to receive parts in a drama that none of us had read, and no one knew what character he or she would play. We were going to be together in close proximity for four weeks, and if we loathed each other there would be no means of escape.

Four were Falkland Islanders. I had already heard about Annie Bonner from Kelly. Elsie and Alf Lee had come over on the same January sailing for him to undergo a cataract operation in England. It was 100 per cent successful and he was returning to Stanley a very happy man, with his sight restored. Then there was a couple named Barnes—and I mention Sid Barnes with great sadness, for within a week of reaching the Falklands he met with an accident and died. Now, with this tragic fate unknown, he and his wife Roz were glowing with excitement and optimism for their future life. Roz had never seen the islands, but Sid had been born and brought up there.

He left as a boy to go to sea and was returning after a thirty-three year absence to take up a job as mechanic on one of the Falkland Islands Trading Company's farms at Port Stephens. The fourth woman was Vivienne Perkins. She told me she was in the W.R.N.S., and, after being in Malta and Tripoli, she had developed a taste for wandering so in 1966 applied for a secretarial job in Stanley. She loved being there and was sorry to leave when her contract expired. Now she had obtained a post with the F.I.C. (Falkland Islands Trading Company, and always referred to as the 'Company', or by its initials) and was delighted to be returning to Stanley where she had made many friends.

Then came the seven hovercraft men—Lieutenant-Commander Peebles, Lieutenant Glennie, and five others selected for special ability in radio or mechanical knowledge. The S.R.N. 6 hovercraft had only been based at Stanley for two years, and, according to the published 1968 report, it had "transformed communications in the Islands by carrying mail and urgent messages to remote farms. It also completed a voyage of nearly one thousand kilometres around the Falklands, partly through gale force winds and three metre waves on exposed coast." I was often to see it dashing up and down Stanley harbour, churning up the water by its high speed. The local nickname for it was 'the hoover-craft', for nearly every housewife had a Hoover cleaner and a Hoover washing-machine. I do not know what my friends on the A.E.S. thought of this joking appellation when they got to hear of it. Now, they were intensely serious about the year's work ahead, anxious to meet the colleagues whom they were relieving, and eager to learn all they could about life on the islands from Annie Bonner, the Lees, Sid Barnes and Vivienne Perkins. Finally, there was Eric Newton, owner of a watch and clock business in Ipswich and fiancé of one of the nursing sisters at King Edward VII Memorial Hospital in Stanley. Naomi was on a two-year government contract, of which she had only completed one quarter. She and Eric became engaged just before she sailed, and he was going out to marry her and stay until he could bring her home. In the meantime he put a manager in charge of the business.

We sailed at ten o'clock that evening. An hour before, the hold was battened down, the derricks lowered, and the gangways drawn up, so that to all intents and purposes we were separated from land and were only waiting for the tide. At last A.E.S. slowly began to manœuvre out of the dock. First she turned in the narrow space, and as we glided past the quayside a van drove up with an urgent parcel, which to our amusement was hauled on board by a rope that was thrown to the van driver. We were all on deck to watch the departure and Chief Steward Kelly said to me, "Twenty-eight days! Yes, you here on this ship for twenty-eight days." It turned out to be thirty, for we were delayed at Las Palmas while the water-distilling machine was repaired and we encountered a heavy gale when we got within 800 miles of the Falklands.

Las Palmas was our only port of call. This was always the case on the outward journey when A.E.S. took on enough oil to last her for seventeen thousand miles; to Stanley, from Stanley to London, and from London to Las Palmas, with a visit to Rotterdam for overhaul every time she returned from the South Atlantic. So after the call at Las Palmas we would go straight down the ocean, from one end of the globe to the other, following a direct route to the Falklands. This would take about a month in a cargo ship of 1,200 gross tonnage, the highest speed of A.E.S. being 12½ knots per hour. Liners going from Southampton to Montevideo and other South American ports were far far larger and capable of far greater speed. Naturally it cost twice the amount to travel in one of them.

Economy and the wish to sample a long voyage on a cargo boat led me to book my return passage on her without hesitation, but I did consider going out the other—and more usual—way. However I was alarmed at the possibility of being obliged to wait in Montevideo before I could sail on to Stanley with only fifty pounds in foreign currency, and I feared this would not go far in a Latin American country. The British currency restrictions then in force did not affect the Falklands, one of our colonies and using sterling. My bank was able to send money to cover my stay there.

Years ago when similar restrictions operated, I had a holiday in Norway, spent more than I intended in Oslo, and reached Bergen with a dangerously low supply of kroner, and still had forty-eight hours before my ship left for England. Once on board the *Venus* I should be all right as I had my ticket, while when

I reached Newcastle I could obtain money from friends, but meanwhile I had to exist for two days. Only too vividly I can remember hoarding every kroner to meet hotel, bed and break-fast bill. I dared not do any sightseeing that required money, so I walked and walked, feeding in the cheapest-looking cafés or buying sandwiches and eating them on a free bench in the free park.

I was not running the risk of finding myself in the same situation again, so I decided to make both outward and return journeys by this direct ship, the A.E.S. In one way this is regrettable because I should have liked to see even a little of South America. Actually the £50 limit was removed at the end of 1969, but I was due to leave Stanley quite soon and it was too late to change. As I have already explained, the *Darwin* was fully booked by then.

The name A.E.S. mystified me until I discovered that the owner, a Dane, had a number of cargo vessels and it was his practice to call them all by initials of members of his family, the surname being Sørensen. A.E.S. was registered at Svenborg, Denmark, in 1957 and was chartered by the F.I.C. She was about 350 feet in length, quite two-thirds being given over to cargo, but the passenger accommodation was comfortable and we had the run of the ship. Everything was very informal. The captain mixed with us, joining in our games of Scrabble and Mah Jong in the evenings, or playing darts with us on deck. His English was excellent.

After leaving Las Palmas we saw no land for twenty-two days. We were as effectively cut-off from the rest of the world as if we were sealed in a space capsule and orbiting around the moon. Thrown together like this, we passengers developed a family intimacy that contributed enormously to enjoyment of the voyage. We had nothing to do all day but read, sleep, eat and talk. How we talked! Five people knew the Falkland Islands, ten people were eager to learn all they could about them.

Of those five, Annie Bonner was a marvellous *raconteur*. She was a merry good-humoured woman, keenly observant, and very kind. Except for two visits to England, she had spent her seventy years on the Falklands, but in different parts of the Camp as well as in Stanley so she knew personally, or by repute, everyone on the Falklands, and she described people and places vividly. Sid Barnes revelled in swopping recollections with Annie, though his memories were of thirty-three years earlier. I remember her describing picnics she had enjoyed on Kidney Island, now a bird sanctuary, where two kinds of penguins breed—the jackass that nests in burrows and the rockhopper, or 'rockie', that makes rough 'nests' on the ground. Penguin eggs were delicious to eat, declared Annie. You boiled one for fifteen minutes, plunged it into cold water to set the opaque white, peeled off the shell, sliced the egg and ate it with bread and butter. I had several chances to sample penguin eggs but could never bring myself to do so. They are used a good deal on the Falklands. I remember being asked to stay for supper at a Stanley house and the hostess was going to cook scrambled eggs on toast.

"What kind of egg would you like?" she asked me. "Hen, goose or penguin?"

Food on the A.E.S. was partly Danish and partly English. We had an English breakfast of bacon, egg, toast, butter, marmalade, but with the addition of cheese, while coffee was always served. Twelve o'clock lunch was the typical Scandinavian assortment of hors d'ouvres and cold meats. At three o'clock we had coffee and cake. Then the 5.30 dinner was a mixture of both nation's cooking—excellent soups made from Danish recipes; roasts, stews, curries, etc., with potatoes and vegetables; tinned fruit with blancmange or ice-cream. Only for a week after leaving Las Palmas did we have fresh fruit, Kelly having bought a supply of oranges and bananas while were were in port.

On the seventh day after leaving London we reached Las Palmas and waited at the harbour entrance for a pilot. It was a gloriously sunny day and the sea the colour of cobalt blue. We were all on deck waiting to see the pilot arrive, and Lieutenant-Commander Peebles (Tony, or, as the men called him, 'Boss') explained the meaning of the four flags that were flying. There was the Spanish (out of courtesy), a striped blue (indicating pilot required), a yellow (customs officer to come on board), and finally the Danish (showing the ship's nationality). Tony said the Danish flag dated back to the eleventh century and was the oldest in the world.

Lord Chalfont's visit to the Falkland Islands in November 1968

8th December, anniversary of the Battle of the Falkland Islands and a public holiday. The governor stands outside the Town Hall, ready to take the salute when the local defence force marches past

Government House, Stanley

Stanley's junior and infant school

Owing to shipping congestion we did not get a vacant berth until late at night, and immediately oil pumping began. This was finished about 5 a.m. when we moved out to the middle of the harbour, to save cost of heavy dues, and anchored for men to come and collect the defective part of the water machine and repair it on shore. I saw the boat arrive and watched it leave, the men going over the side of the ship, climbing down a swaying rope ladder, then jumping several feet into a wobbling boat, for there was quite a heavy swell. Captain Svendsen said he had arranged for a motor launch from Las Palmas to collect us passengers at 1 p.m. and we could have five and a half hours on shore, the launch bringing us back in time for six o'clock when he hoped to sail. I was pleased about this until I realized I should have to do the same as the workmen, go down the rope ladder and jump, but I dare not say so and comforted myself with the thought that I should have Tony and Ian to help me over the side, and the others—Alex, Bungay, John, Mike and Phil—to catch me when I jumped from ladder to launch. However, I was spared this ordeal. Either the workmen never delivered the captain's message to owner of launch, or he was not going to miss his afternoon siesta—anyway, it failed to arrive.

The next fortnight was very pleasant. We spent the mornings lounging on the boat deck, talking, and petting two sheepdogs who were being brought to the Falklands to rejoin their owners. After lunch most of us retired to our cabins to sleep away the time until three o'clock coffee, followed by more chat and sunbathing or a dip in the canvas swimming pool. It was too small to do more than three strokes. Evenings were spent in playing games or watching films. The films were mostly very poor, of old vintage, and with the addition of Danish captions to make them intelligible to the crew. Chief Steward Kelly enlivened us with his jokes. Outside his cabin he had a canary in a cage and it used to sing joyfully in the sunshine.

I saw a good deal of the Barnes and listened to plans for their new life at Port Stephens. Roz was a farmer's daughter so knew something about sheep farming and loved country life. Sid had been captain of an English coastal vessel until Roz noticed his tiredness after each voyage and wanted him to find a less exacting job. One day he asked her if she would consider going to

c

live on the Falklands. It had always been his dream to return to the islands of his birth. Roz was only too eager to back him up in fulfilment of that dream, so they contacted the F.I.C. London office and he obtained this job of farm mechanic. Although the pay was only £45 a month, Roz declared they would be as well-off as in England earning six times that amount. They were to have a house provided, rent free, as well as free meat, free milk, free butter, and income tax on the Falklands was very much lower than in Britain. Like me, she was in an escapist mood, scorning contemporary British way of life with its dependence on the Welfare State and its obsession with television. Roz said over and over again how thankful she was to get away from it all, and, though I could not echo that as a permanancy, I welcomed the temporary respite. I felt that on these isolated islands the people would all be fine characters, rugged and indomitable, not flabby nor spoilt by mass media entertainment. At a Falkland Islands reunion of exiles in London, Roz had been disgusted at a few people who preferred life in Britain. It was because they were ready to abandon the struggle against wind and weather and general hardship—so we both thought then—that folk who felt like that settled in Britain, and surely there must be very few of them. With scorn Roz repeated the words of one woman, "Give me a bag of toffees and the telly and I am happy." I thought it dreadful too, little dreaming that on the return voyage I would be yearning to see television again.

There was always the sea to look at, and the possibility of whales spouting in the distance or birds flying by the ship. There were flying fish, Cape pigeons, and, the most awe-inspiring of birds, the albatross. The two sheepdogs were terrified when one first glided above the boat deck, but quickly got used to this happening several times a day. Each albatross seemed to gaze at us with anger as though we had no right to be on the sea where he and his kind reigned with supreme majesty, and I would look spellbound at the magnificent wing-span.

It is an old custom on ships to hold a special ceremony when passing the equator. A fictitious Neptune, god of the sea, demands penalties from those who cannot prove they have previously undergone initiation rites on 'crossing the line'. Today it has been banned on many liners because of complaints from outraged passengers at being ducked in a swimming pool, and other horseplay, and the only time I had witnessed it was on a ship bound for South Africa. Then it degenerated into a fancy dress show by certain members of the crew, while passengers watched from an upper deck. But I believe it is still held on naval vessels according to customary tradition, with everyone taking part and much boisterous behaviour. Anyway, our hovercraft friends insisted on having the real thing and Captain Svendsen was quite willing.

Tony Peebles put up a notice in the lounge, and it was set out in beautiful script.

Apprehension of Dissidents and Illegal Entry into any part of the Kingdom.
ROYAL PROCLAMATION
In so far as it pleases His Most Royal Majesty Neptunus Rex, Ruler of the Seven Seas and of All Deeps, Head and Father of all inhabitants thereof, from Mermen and Mermaids, Whales and Dolphins, Fishes and Shells, Sea Sprites and Water Wonders, to lowly and no less mean slimy creatures on their Oceans' very floors—I am Commanded to give you His Welcome, and further to Demand that you prepare yourselves to receive His Magnificent Presence and Court, to answer any charges that will be laid, and to present your papers.

Be Ye Ready in all respects and in attendance at 16.00 today, in position 2° 30′ S, 30° 15′ W.

Given under My Hand, to date, Wednesday, 24th September, 1969

Neptune's Herald of the Booming Conch, Crabs and Barnacles.

We actually crossed the equator on 23rd September, but this fact was ignored, and a day late we gathered together in the right-hand footway on the cargo deck. On the hold itself were thrones for Neptune and his queen, acted by the First Engineer and Roz. Tony was herald and he announced their approach. The Queen was wonderfully attired in a bathing costume covered with gauzy blue tunic, and she wore a wig of red un-ravelled rope, the 'locks' being held in place by plastic clothes pegs. Tony wore a red towelled dressing-gown and peculiar plastic hat. The Tritons (Neptune's trumpeters in classical mythology) had long flowing skirts of the same unplaited rope. Two other stock characters in the ceremony were the barber and the surgeon, and they had white overalls covered with daubs of paint.

The first victim was the blond curly-haired 'Al-ann', who bowed obediently to Neptune and was made to drink some mixture handed to him, then kiss the queen's foot, sit in the surgeon's chair and have a salted fish pushed into his mouth, then proceed to the barber for soaping, lathering and a pretended shave with dummy razor. His ordeal ended with a ducking in the swimming pool. 'Al-ann' smiled through it all, but some who followed did not submit so easily. One of the deck hands seized the fish and flung it overboard. Another wriggled and fought with the Tritons and nearly pushed them into the pool. Those of us who had been in the southern hemisphere before were exempt—except for saluting Neptune and his queen —but not the queen herself. This was Roz's first crossing of the line so at the end she jumped into the pool, became entangled with her false flowing locks and had to be rescued by Neptune himself.

Afterwards certificates were issued. They were beautifully painted by Tony and showed a tiny map of the world with route to the Falklands, a picture of A.E.S. with Danish flag against a background of East Falkland, and two penguins. Underneath them was a grizzly-haired Neptune holding a fish in his right hand and a trident in the other. At the bottom was a huge fish and a mermaid sitting on a rock. Between pictures was the script—in Danish, but Captain Svendsen gave us a translation. He signed each certificate to prove that the owner had undergone the traditional ceremony.

We left London on 8th September and had calm seas for the remainder of that month, save for an occasional swell, but on 1st October the temperature dropped appreciably and the A.E.S. began to roll, then to pitch, as she battled against a strong southerly wind blowing from Cape Horn. We were in the Roaring Forties, the latitudes of seas so dreaded in the old sailing-ship era. Rails were fixed round the dining-room tables and clothes damped to keep dishes steady, but even so meals were chaotic as soup sloshed about and the very act of spreading butter on bread was a difficult feat. Our young steward 'Al-ann' was skilled at balancing as he carried food from galley to dining-room, and quite unconcerned over any mishap. When a blancmange slid from dish to floor, he cleared up the gooey mess in a minute, and brought tinned fruit instead. One day Kelly was unable to get to the fo'castle where the stores were kept and curry had to be served without rice. Speed was so reduced that we would obviously be overdue in reaching Stanley, and I told Kelly I hoped he had enough supplies to feed us for the extra days. "Plenty of potatoes," he assured me.

Looking through windows that faced the bows, the sea appeared terrifying. A.E.S. would rise to ride a massive mountainous wave, then plunge into a foaming trough of blue-green water, her prow emerging again to encounter the next onset. Telegraph poles on the cargo deck broke loose from their lashings and when two seamen went to secure them, the two men got soaked to the skin. More alarming was a frightful crash that occurred on the port side late one evening, caused by the falling of a companionway that led from one deck to another. Some of us were trying to play Scrabble but without success because the letters slid all over the board, and we jumped up on hearing this awful noise. It sounded as if something far worse had happened.

Sid Barnes told us that when he first went to sea in 1936, it was in an Antarctic sailing ship. Coming from South Georgia to Stanley, she was blown past the Falkland Islands and could do nothing but let herself be driven north by the gale. It did not cease until they were nearly level with Montevideo, so they had to return 1,000 miles to reach their destination. We were thankful to be in a ship with engine power. Although our speed was reduced to a couple of knots per hour—if that—at least we were set in the right direction and not going backwards. Annie Bonner tried to cheer us up by saying we should soon be in radio communication with Stanley. We were allowed into the wheelhouse, and I was told I should hear our captain trying to make contact by air.

"This is A.E.S. calling. Fleetwing, Fleetwing, can you hear me?" Fleetwing was the cable code name of the F.I.C. office.

On 6th October the sea was still rather rough, but the waves were gradually subsiding and Captain Svendsen said he hoped to get into Stanley in another two or three days. Our speed was now 8 knots. He had been speaking to Stanley, and it was cold there with snow storms. The month of October is the equivalent of April in the northern hemisphere so it was spring in the Falklands. "Still cold, very cold," he remarked. "Maybe ice on the sea."

Next morning he told me at breakfast he had received a radio message saying that the Ship Hotel was unable to take me but accommodation had been found by British Antarctic Survey, and Mr. Ted Clapp would meet the A.E.S. and take me to lodgings. It was utterly beyond my comprehension why British Antarctic Survey was concerning itself, and it was only after talking to Mr. Clapp that I discovered Mrs. Sandra Gipps' husband had written to him about me. That accounted for the mysterious paragraph in her letter.

Annie Bonner was very relieved by this news. She confessed she was worried about my accommodation because in a letter from the Falklands she learnt that the Ship Hotel was sold to a Mr. King, who was going to close it while it was being altered and modernized.

"A fine place he hopes to make of it, by all accounts. In Stanley they are already calling it Des King's Hilton, but it won't be ready until next year, so I didn't see how you could stay there. But you'll be all right, Margaret, with Ted Clapp and Jean looking after you. Jean is a Falkland girl and her mother is a great friend of mine, and they've got a lovely house. Ted is in charge of B.A.S.—that's what they call British Antarctic Survey—office in Stanley."

3

Through the Narrows

TWENTY-FOUR hours later, and doing 9 knots, we began to hope we might reach Stanley that evening; and at half-past three I rushed on deck when I heard land was in sight. Two dark humps on the horizon—that was my first glimpse of the islands I had travelled more than 8,000 miles to see.

We were then about 30 miles away from Port William. This forms an outer harbour to the inner harbour of Stanley, the latter being like a great floating dock. The two are connected by The Narrows, a channel only 300 yards wide and about 5½ fathoms in depth. My excitement increased as we drew closer to land, and on the right I could see hills with curved contours, smooth like circles of halved globes against the sky. Their slopes and the moorland below were green, white and mahogany. The green grass was broken by outcrops of quartz rock, and the dark brown patches were diddle dee, a plant with fruit akin to our bilberry and growing in great profusion all over the Falklands. The scientific name is *Empetrum rubrum*. It reaches 1½ inches in height, is easily ignited, and produces edible red berries that Islanders use for making jam or jelly, slightly bitter in taste. There is a local belief that if one eats diddle dee one will return to the Falkland Islands.

As we sailed along I saw what appeared to be a wide silvery river with sprawling tributaries flowing down a hill and guessed this to be a stone run, or stream of stone, a phenomenon that has impressed every traveller, including Charles Darwin.

"In some places," he writes, "a continuous stream of these fragments followed up the course of the valley, and even extended to the very crest of the hill. On these crests huge masses, exceeding in dimensions any small building, seemed to stand arrested in their headlong course: there, also, the curved strata of the archways lay piled on each other, like the ruins of some vast and ancient cathedral."

The origin of the stone runs has not yet been satisfactorily explained. According to one theory they may be due to soil and loose rock debris becoming saturated with water, then under gravitational influence flowing along the land's surface. This happened when an Ice Age gave way to warmer climatic conditions. Some geologists disagree. One objection to this is that solifluction can be seen today in arctic and antarctic regions, yet, according to D. H. Malling, "there are no known examples of stone runs of similar size in similar topography, which are in the process of accumulation".

Alf Lee, who was standing beside me, pointed out the wreck of the *Great Britain* in Sparrow Cove. This renowned ship was in the news when I left home because of a campaign to raise £150,000 to tow her back to Britain, repair her, refit her as the mammoth Victorian liner that she was once, and recoup the money spent by putting her on show with suitable admittance charge. 'The Iron Wonder', as she used to be called, was the first big vessel to be built of iron and the first to be driven by screw propeller. She was designed by Brunel. Her tonnage of 3,500 was considered stupendous in 1843, while her sixty-four staterooms and 1,200 yards of carpet heralded a new era of luxury in passenger sea transport. Intended for the Liverpool to New York crossing, she was not a success, and in 1850 she was sold. The new owners refitted her for the Australian emigrant trade, and between 1852 and 1875 she called at least once at Stanley for coaling. Towards the end of her career she was solely concerned with cargo and had been turned into a sailing ship. Her six masts, named after days of the week, were reduced to three, and her iron hulk was sheathed in wood. In 1886 she was badly damaged by a gale when rounding the Horn, limped into Stanley harbour, was condemned as beyond repair, so there she remained and was used as a store by the F.I.C. The company abandoned her in 1933 and she was towed into Sparrow Cove, where she was lying when I passed in the A.E.S.

In Stanley I heard much doubt expressed about the project of taking her back to Britain to become a floating museum and show-piece. General opinion said she was in a pitiful state and this notion of reclaiming her had come twenty years too late. However experts had been sent out from Britain to examine her and their report was favourable, so preparations for towing were supposed to start early in 1970.* First she was to be filled with some kind of plastic foam to prevent her from breaking in two on the homeward journey. Certainly she looked a very derelict wreck as viewed from the A.E.S. deck that evening.

There was now land on both sides and I went to join Sid and Roz who were on the port side. Roz and I gasped at the soft shades of colour—pale lime green, silvery white, dove grey, light mauve, and these pastels contrasted strongly with the dark brown of the diddle dee patches. "But it is beautiful!" We kept exclaiming this and I marvelled how some former travellers, notably Darwin, could have been unenthusiastic. As regards Darwin, he was a notoriously bad sailor so probably was recovering from sea sickness he endured while the *Beagle* sailed to the Falklands, and this soured his outlook.

A.E.S. stopped her engines in the outer harbour, before entering The Narrows, the channel that led to the inner harbour. Sid thought Captain Svendsen must be waiting for instructions from Stanley, since it was after six o'clock and work at the jetty would have ceased for the day. We might have to anchor and wait until morning. Then Sid started to point out where warships were stationed when the Battle of the Falkland Islands began on 8th December 1914. The date is still observed as a public holiday, and Sid said that when he was a schoolboy in Stanley they always had a lesson on this famous engagement. In it Britain defeated the German squadron in the South Atlantic and avenged a defeat she had sustained a month earlier at Coronel (Chile).

On 7th December several battle cruisers, including the flagship H.M.S. *Invincible,* arrived at Stanley to take on coal. German ships guessed their destination and followed at a discreet distance, so the British were really taken unawares. Some ships were in the outer harbour and others coaling off Stanley. One of them, *Canopus* received a signal from the look-out post

* The *Great Britain* was successfully brought back to England in 1970.

on Sappers Hill to warn the enemy's approach, and they all got up steam. The battle soon began.

Sid did not get any further with his narrative because the A.E.S. revved up her engines and began to move slowly towards The Narrows, the 300-yard channel and gateway to the inner harbour where lies the Falklands' only town, her capital. The sun was now low in the sky, though not yet actually setting, and the shimmering placid water was crowded with gulls, shearwaters, skuas and other birds unknown to me. Straight ahead, darkly purple against the horizon, was a line of hills, but these had sharp pointed shapes, not rounded, and two were conical. Sid told me those peaks were called the Twin Sisters.

I had come across several impressions of Stanley in my reading. One traveller called it "a queer old sleepy" place; another, "a small grey town beneath windy skies . . . unattractive at first sight"; and a third wrote of "white cottages and light frame-houses scattered somewhat irregularly on the slope of a hill". I expected it to resemble a gloomy South Wales mining village or a drab Lancashire cotton town, only far smaller, but now I found myself confronted by a panorama of brightly painted houses—red, blue or green—each one obviously surrounded by a garden. It was as if I were looking through a kaleidoscope. I remembered my first sight of Reyjavik, the capital of Iceland, from a ship, and Stanley was equally colourful. So this was the British Commonwealth's most southerly town, a cathedral city, and a capital of only 1,000 inhabitants.

Stanley was established in 1843, and 'established' is the most suitable word for what was an artificial creation. After the British flag was again planted on Falkland soil in 1833, Port Soledad reverted to its former French name of Port Louis, which it has continued to bear in spite of Lieutenant-Governor Moody's attempt to call it Anson. Today Port Louis is one of the many sheep farm settlements and barely fifty people live there.

When colonization began in earnest the British Admiralty favoured a more convenient site for the settlement. Ships often had to wait for a favourable wind before they could enter or leave Berkeley Sound where Port Louis was situated. There was a harbour called Jackson's further south and this had not the same disadvantage. Moreover, there was excellent anchorage in both outer and inner harbours. A site was chosen on the south side of the inner, and the new settlement was named Stanley after Edward Geoffrey Smith Stanley, fourteenth Earl of Derby, and then Secretary of State for the Colonies. About 100 people, mostly gauchos and sealers and whalers, were transferred there by Lieutenant-General Moody in 1843.

In 1849 thirty pensioners were brought from Chelsea Royal Hospital, the hospital for veteran soldiers that was founded by Charles II. Many were in their forties, and old by mid-Victorian standards, but there were eleven between the ages of 30 and 40, and even one of 25. Miss Madge Biggs, the Stanley librarian, showed me a list of their names as recorded in the 1851 census and she marked seven whose descendants still lived on the Falklands. She was proud to be one of them. Some of the pensioners settled happily, but others disliked the grim life, or their war wounds prevented them from the hard labour needed in digging gardens and growing vegetables. Those who could not make good returned to Britain, but the others remained as permanent colonists. They had brought wives and children. Then, in 1858, they were joined by a garrison of thirty-five marines, also with families. There was plenty of work in ship repairing and in selling provisions to passing ships, for Stanley was becoming an important port of call. In 1851 the Falkland Islands Trading Company was formed and was soon establishing sheep farming in the Camp, bringing in both men and stock.

After crawling through The Narrows, we steered for a jetty, but our progress was slow and lights were beginning to appear in houses and in the streets. The town was larger than I expected, and the sloping ground on which it was built was steeper. Several people were waiting on the jetty where we tied up. Annie Bonner and Vivienne Perkins recognized friends, Elsie and Alf Lee saw one of their daughters, and there were loud whoops from hovercraft men who had come to greet their relief mates. "Welcome to the Falklands! Did you have a good trip? We don't sail until the 20th so don't know how we are going to squash in you fellows at Moody Brook. Some will have to sleep in tents." Sid Barnes distinguished two cousins whom he had not expected to be there and were unknown to Roz. They were calling out an invitation to stay at their house. Eric was waving to his Naomi. I should have felt very forlorn if I had not recognized her companion, Bridie Rooney, also a nursing sister and whom I had met previously on the island of St. Helena. A mutual friend had written to tell her I was on my way to the Falklands, and as soon as the Medical Officer of Health and the Immigration authorities cleared the ship, she rushed on board with the rest and welcomed me with her usual Irish warmth.

Kelly came to tell me Mr. Clapp was waiting 'with his jeep', so I had to leave. I was still perplexed over the concern B.A.S. was displaying. Mr. Clapp greeted me, took my cases off Kelly, and put them into his Land-Rover. I was soon to discover that this type of vehicle was the usual means of motor transport, for ordinary cars could only be used on the 12 miles of road in and about Stanley. As we started to drive away, some official opened the door and wished me a happy stay on the islands, a very kind gesture I thought.

We bounced off the jetty, skidded round a corner, and chugged up a hill as perpendicular as any in a South Wales valley town, while Mr. Clapp explained that Mr. Gipps had written asking him to look after me, so when he found the 'Ship' was closing he looked for somewhere I could stay. He apologized for not taking me to his own house as his wife and little son were ill with influenza, but he had fixed me up with the Mays in Glasgow Road and I would be very comfortable there. Mr. Gipps had also told him I wanted to visit the Camp, so he had written to a number of sheep farm managers and would give me their letters of reply if I called at his office to-morrow. Then we stopped. I got out and found myself shaking hands with Heather and Willie May.

First impressions in a strange place are usually confusing. I was utterly bewildered by the sudden transition from ship to land, from the A.E.S., so familiar after a month's voyage, to this Stanley house where I should be staying for a few months. My first reaction was how bright and tasteful! I had expected Falkland Island homes to be furnished in Victorian style and cluttered with antimacassars, aspidistras, pot-pourri, even whatnots, but this was modern and the colourings green and gold. A glowing peat fire was burning in the sitting-room grate, and the effect was warm and cheerful and welcoming. Soon I was revelling in the first good cup of tea I had had for weeks.

Excellent as was the food on A.E.S., the Danes could not make tea that came up to English standards.

Turning to my host and hostess, I saw they were somewhere in their thirties. They had no children. Later I learnt both were born and grew up in the Camp. Heather had lived on two different islands off West Falkland—Carcass and West Point, and could do any job on a sheep farm. Willie had worked as a shepherd at five settlements—Roy Cove, Hill Cove, Chartres, Carcass and West Point. Now he was a storekeeper for B.A.S., but although he enjoyed life in Stanley, I felt Heather's heart was still in the Camp and that she missed country and farm. She was an excellent cook and housekeeper, and Willie was kindness itself in taxi-ing me around in his Land-Rover or, to be correct, his Gipsy-Arguson. I am sure I could not have stayed in a pleasanter or more comfortable home.

I went to bed completely exhausted, unable to believe I was no longer tossing about on the ocean, but I woke quite restored to normality. Mr. Clapp had given Willie the morning off to take me about, so, after a late breakfast of bacon and egg—the egg from one of Heather's own back-garden fowls—I was driven to the F.I.C. office. When I finished my business there, we went to Government House so that I could sign the visitors' book, for until one does that one will not receive official invitations. The Governor and his wife were away in England. A new Colonial Secretary was acting governor in his absence.

On the way I saw the Barnes and stopped to speak to them. Sid was flying by Beaver plane to Port Stephens the next day to start his new job, but Roz was waiting to see their furniture safely on board the *Forrest*. She was a small government ship that carried cargo round the islands. Sid intended to get the house ready and at least have beds put up before Roz joined him. For the week he was alone at Port Stephens he would sleep at the cookhouse—a feature of every sheep farm settlement where the unmarried shepherds are boarded. Roz said we must meet while she was still in Stanley. "And, of course, you must come to Port Stephens and stay with us as soon as we are settled and straight."

I signed the book at Government House. Then Willie took me to the B.A.S. office where I found Mr. Clapp was away ill. He too had caught the influenza. But one of his clerks handed me the folder of letters I was supposed to have. "They are from Camp managers and Mr. Clapp said on the phone that would you deal with them as you thought fit."

Willie went to work in the afternoon and I started to explore Stanley—not that there was a great deal to explore. I remembered one of Annie Bonner's stories about a local girl who went to Canada and married a millionaire with a passion for walking. They came on a visit to her home, but he was most disappointed to find he could not get enough exercise in Stanley as he said he could walk from one end to the other in fifteen minutes.

That afternoon there was no wind, which was unusual, and I was struck by the extraordinary freshness of the air. It gave one a feeling of exhilaration. The weather was warm, like an April day in Britain, but such a mild spell in October was rare in the Falklands. Most gardens had a few daffodils coming into bloom, while the gorse hedges were gloriously golden. Everything stood out sharply in the clear atmosphere.

The plan of the town was simple. Ross Road, named after an antarctic explorer who visited the islands in 1842, ran beside the harbour and became Ross Road West after it passed Government House. From this main highway, several streets led upwards—Hebe Street, Philomel Street, Dean Street and Villiers Street—and crossing them but parallel with Ross Road were three more thoroughfares. One was called after Fitzroy, who commanded the *Beagle*, and another was Davis Street after John Davis, captain of the *Desire*. Later I came across Drury Street and Pioneer Row Cottages where the Chelsea Pensioners lived, though any of their houses still standing must have been modernized and altered out of recognition. There is a record of No. 12 Drury Street being given to Thomas Dowers, a pensioner who was 36 when he reached the Falklands, and he had the cottage as a reward "for services performed" and "at a yearly rental of one peppercorn".

Gorse is not a native plant, neither is macrocarpa which was brought from South America and also forms hedges in Stanley gardens. As for trees—yes there were trees, but of course imported and carefully protected against the fierce cutting winds. Most of those in the capital have come from Chile and were planted during World War I, but I never discovered if that was the history of a tall monkey-puzzle tree—the only one of its kind that I saw on the islands. It stood in front of Stanley Cottage, which was not a cottage but a large house.

Houses were mainly built of wood with corrugated iron roofs, and painted in bright colours. Bungalows were quite common. There were some attractive modern houses, one of the most charming being a pre-fabricated one from Sweden, reputed to have cost its owner £7,000—a large sum for property in Stanley. Most palatial was the 100-year-old mansion, Stanley House, the residence of the F.I.C. Colonial Manager. It looked so imposing and stood in such well-kept grounds that I took it to be Government House until I found that was a sprawling red-brick affair much further along Ross Road. Also of red brick, and looking incongruous amongst the white and yellow wooden houses, were the four Jubilee Villas built in 1887, the year of Queen Victoria's golden jubilee. They were old-fashioned, with long narrow halls and bay windows, but must have been costly to build as, even then, each brick was 1s. 6d. Besides a garage, there was always at least one additional shed, and I, in my ignorance, thought this must be to accommodate a second car. However it was to hold peat, the only fuel found in the Falklands; it is vital to have a large stock of it before winter begins.

The dozen shops were scattered about Ross Road, John Street and Fitzroy Road. They were scattered, not collected in a shopping centre. Some were just in private houses and approached by a path through the front garden. As for window-dressing, that was non-existent, there being little need for publicity. Everyone knew that a few days after the arrival of A.E.S. fresh stocks of goods would appear in the shops. Most of them dealt in the same things—groceries, cameras, radios, sweets, clothes, and it amazed me to see that half of them claimed to sell millinery. I thought that extraordinary in a place where few women wore hats, only headscarves and hoods, but I found that in the Falklands the term millinery is used for ladies coats, dresses, even underwear.

The Falkland Islands Company store, described in one guide as the local "Selfridges", had recently changed its name from West Store to Newest Store. A month before my arrival a new manager introduced self-service into the food department, and customers were still unaccustomed to the innovation. That first afternoon I took a basket from the pile and wandered around, not because I needed to buy anything but out of curiosity to see the stock and compare prices with Britain. In most cases they were lower, particularly wines, spirits and cigarettes, because of the absence of purchase tax. Freight charges made everything slightly higher than it would have otherwise been, but still cheaper than at home. Everything seemed to be imported— bacon from England, butter from New Zealand, even dehydrated tripe from Argentina! There were also tins of mutton stew from a Liverpool firm—and this in the sheep-producing Falklands! I expected to see commodities like bacon, butter, and cheese brought from the Camp, but there was no sign of such local produce. This was explained to me later on. Then I went into the hardware and the 'millinery' departments. There were some ready-made clothes for women, but I learnt in time that it was the habit to buy material as soon as it arrived by A.E.S., then send to Britain for paper pattern of style one fancied— possibly gleaned from a three-month-old magazine—and as the application for pattern and pattern itself would take several weeks, one could not start making a new dress for a couple of months.

In a guide to Stanley sent me by the then Colonial Secretary, the F.I.C. store was described as having a "beauty salon", so I never anticipated difficulty over getting my hair done; but the beauty salon was closed and the only trained hairdresser gone from the Falklands. Like other women, I was forced to let my hair grow until I returned to Britain, and felt an untidy sight all the time I was away. My first day back in London, I rushed to a hair stylist, explaining I had been on some islands near the South Pole where there was no such civilized amenity as a ladies' hairdresser. Most women, even colonial officers' wives, did not seem to mind, but then there was little concern about a smart appearance. The wind blew off make-up. It was comfortable and snug to slop around in trousers, padded anorak and headscarf. Although I put on a fur coat for church, it was not really 'done'. Kelpers were so hardy they scorned furs.

One evening Heather and Willie were taking me to visit some friends, Russell and 'Tricia Johnson. It was abominably cold and the wind was bitter. I said in desperation, "I don't care what you think but I must wear my fur coat." Willie parked the vehicle outside the Johnson bungalow in Ross Road West.

One of the cross streets in Stanley

The memorial to the Battle of the Falkland Islands, Stanley

Weddell Island: *(above)* the settlement and *(below)* the manager's
daughter, Teena Ferguson

Then we walked along an exposed concrete path and up steps to the front door where the usually friendly labrador, Dusty, came to greet us. The fur coat evidently gave her the notion that I was a strange animal, for she barked angrily, and it was only after Russell dragged her aside that I could enter the house. Once I had taken off my coat, Dusty came to me, wagging her tail and asking to be petted.

4

The Way of Life in Stanley

I WENT to the Falklands because the islands interested me and because I was curious to see how people lived and adapted themselves to the isolation, although I did not realize how great that isolation was until I actually got there. I was determined to adjust myself to whatever conditions I found, for this is essential if one wants to penetrate the outer crust. One observes and one assimilates and, moreover, one makes comparisons with other countries, but to understand a place, especially an island, one must become acquainted with the inhabitants and try to see their viewpoint. On the Falklands this was very difficult, something I did not realize at first. Some officials and some Kelpers did all they could to help me, but I discovered others were intensely suspicious of my intentions and that it was said openly in the Colony Club, "What does she mean by coming to write a book about us? Such cheek!" Actually I wished the person who repeated this remark had kept silent. I would have preferred to have remained in ignorance of such an attitude. Only in the course of conversation with a Britisher, who was leaving the islands after a contract had expired, did I realize that being a woman had also been a tremendous handicap.

Then I was up against difficulties of verbal communication. We spoke the same language but actual words did not always mean the same and my experience of life, my entire outlook, was far removed from that of the average Kelper. I could not grasp this at first, for the majority had visited Britain or had relatives there. Then I found that nearly all those who did have a holiday in Britain stayed with friends or relations, or took a house, but did very little sight-seeing. They were not interested in the British way of life, nor even in news from the Mother

Country, although Union Jacks were waving all over the place and "God Save The Queen" was sung on every possible occasion, even at the conclusion of church services. Newspapers and other periodicals were two months old by the time they reached the Falklands. There is no television. People listened on radio sets to the B.B.C. Overseas News, but this dealt chiefly with world affairs rather than British news, and I doubt if the items made much impression on people so cut off, their only link with the outside world being Britain. I remember once being struck by Kelper lack of comprehension regarding different global climatic conditions. It was an unusually pleasant sunny day and some American astronauts were due to splash down thousands of miles away in the Pacific, but in a Stanley shop I heard a Falkland Islander remark, "Good job it is a fine day for these moon men to land."

Neither Kelpers, nor temporary British residents, appeared to take any interest in cultural activities. At social gatherings I found that conversation lagged terribly for there was nothing to talk about—no television programmes, no films, no art, no classical music, very little reading and that usually confined to thrillers and westerns, while news was too out-of-date to be news. In the Camp people wanted to hear the latest Stanley happenings, but in Stanley the reverse did not operate.

It was impossible to grasp the ramifications of Stanley society, intensified by the colonial structure, for of course invitations to Government House were issued in accordance with rules of protocol affecting all crown colonies. But among the bulk of Falkland Islanders, and also among temporary British residents, I found social distinctions that had ceased to exist in this country. The Camp varied. Some settlements were democratic and friendly without any gulf between 'Big House' and the small dwellings. At others I got a different impression, and later I heard from former shepherds, stories that sounded more like the era of Trollope than the year 1969.

The behaviour of some British people with jobs often irritated the Kelpers, partly through unavoidable misunderstandings, but also through stupid indifference to local difficulties. For instance, a man's eighteen months' contract was about to expire and he was booked by his organization, with wife and children, to return the most expensive way, that is to fly from Montevideo.

Therefore his heavy baggage and goods, like record player, children's toys, etc., all had to be crated and sent in advance by A.E.S. This had happened when he came out so when he tried to obtain such a rare commodity as wooden crates he was asked, "Where are the ones you had before?" "Oh, I chopped them up to burn on the kids' Guy Fawkes bonfire." Only people living on an island where there are virtually no trees and where every bit of wood has to be imported can realize the horror of a Falklander at such wanton waste. Kelpers would only use rubbish, or maybe diddle dee, on bonfires.

Then I heard complaints about arrogance shown by some Britishers, who considered they had been sent to the back of beyond and openly said so, regardless of the resentment they aroused. One Falkland Islander even complained to me about the overbearing behaviour of soldiers stationed there in World War II. "They used to treat us like a lot of dirty natives," he said.

I am inclined to think too that the Kelper has an inferiority complex because he feels remote from other places, and this makes real communication of thought hard. One would expect exchange of ideas between two sets of people, both descended from the same British stock, both speaking the same language, to be easy, but it is not.

Television has not yet come to the Falklands but it was the first British colony to have its own broadcasting system of sound radio and this began in 1929, covering Stanley and a small part of East Falkland. In 1942 came the Radio Transmitter (the R.T.) which embraced all the islands. A system of wired rediffusion brings the local radio into the home and the loud-speaker, called the Box, is usually kept switched on, apart from the normal thirty-four to thirty-six and a half hours of broadcasting, because of special announcements. Programmes include local news; music—discs of pop and light orchestra pieces as well as Latin American dances, but never works by classical composers; plays; talks; and "The Archers", which is exceedingly popular and is sent on tapes by the B.B.C. Transcription Service. The tapes are two years old when they reach Stanley. When I was returning home, one of the ship's passengers managed to get London on his set towards the end of the voyage and he listened excitedly when an instalment of "The Archers" began. He thought the gap would be four weeks, from the time he left Stanley, but as it was twenty-five months he was completely fogged by new characters and new happenings.

"Visitors' Box" is a weekly feature. I had only been in Stanley a few days when the Reverend Peter Millam, Senior Chaplain at the Cathedral, escorted me to the studio for an interview. I was asked, "Where have you come from? Why are you here? How long are you going to be here?" Peter wanted to know what kind of a book I intended to write and the titles of books I already had published. Then I was asked to give my first impressions of Stanley.

The studio was very informal and I was introduced to Nadine Campbell, responsible for the programme, and a technician. They sat in the main room from which transmitting took place. It was also the recording-room and a store for discs and tapes, while a glass window looked into the interviewing-room. Peter and I were in the latter, and the technician signalled through the window for us to begin.

On my second visit to the studio I met the head of the service, Mr. Charles Reade. Nadine had kindly promised to run through a tape-recording of a talk I missed, given by the former Administrator of South Georgia. This antarctic island belongs to Britain and used to be a whaling base, but now whaling has ceased. Personnel were evacuated while I was on the Falklands, and B.A.S. was going to use it as an extra base, but the administrator's house and the newly-built Shackleton House for staff were left to become derelict. I was told they were sumptuously furnished and had cost Britain £25,000 a few years previously.

Special odd-hour radio announcements might give times of Beaver flights, passenger lists for planes or ships, new goods on sale in shops and individual messages of general interest. I was struck by Kelper honesty when it was considered worth while to put over the information that someone had lost a sum of money "in an envelope during Tuesday afternoon or Wednesday morning so would finder hand it to. . . ." It seemed marvellous to me that the finder could be so honest, but the Falklands are islands where property and order are respected. If you put a notice on a car for sale asking children not to touch it, they obey.

A usual feature of any small community is that there is no

'keeping oneself to oneself'. Details about a stranger are soon known and his or her actions noticed. As for the telephone I found the personal side of the service quite amusing. Every house in Stanley has a phone for which the householder pays a modest annual rent, but all calls are free. The automatic system is unknown. You turn a handle and ask the operator for the required number, and if you have given the wrong one she tells you so. "I think you've got the wrong number, Miss Taylor," the operator said once. "That is, is you want Mrs. Tony Carey. No 335 is for Mr. Carey's brother." Another time she remarked, "I can't put you through to Joan this morning because she has gone to bed with flu' and she told me she did not want to be disturbed." "You'd better try again in an hour. Mary isn't at home. I've just seen her from the window here and she looked as if she was going shopping."

Falkland Islanders living in Stanley either worked in one of the governmental departments, or for the Company or B.A.S. or E.S.R.O. (European Space Research Organization), or in a shop. Some colonial wives, also B.A.S. and E.S.R.O. ones took jobs, but others were unable to leave their small children so pushed prams about, looking bored and miserable, obviously counting the months or weeks until their departure and hoping their husbands' next posting would be to some sunny clime with a golden beach. Domestic help was almost impossible to get. Even Government House and the hospital had difficulty. There was too much prosperity for Kelper women to take up work that did not attract them. As one housewife told me, and she did not only mean housework, "These are do-it-yourself islands."

For husbands it was gardening and peat cutting during leisure hours in spring and summer, the only two seasons of the year that I was there. Gardening is very, very hard work. The soil never gets really warm so growth of vegetables and flowers is slow, and once the plant appears above ground it needs constant protection from the wind. A gusty morning and some cherished lupins would be dashed down to the ground. Lettuces are pathetically small, but I could not judge their quality of taste for Stanley followed the South American practice of shredding the leaves and thus destroying the flavour. Potatoes are almost impossible to grow in Stanley, though plentiful in the Camp. This is due to eelworm, a pest that attacks the roots and cannot be eradicated, even if the soil is left to lie fallow for seven years. I only heard of one man growing them successfully, but he had cleared his garden of every bit of soil right down to the rock, then got eelworm-free soil from the Camp.

Old and infirm folk were obliged to pay for their peat to be cut, and this cost about £40 a year, but for most Stanley householders it was another do-it-yourself burden, and an absolute necessity unless you were one of the few who had a new house with oil central heating. Peat cutting on the Camp was done on a communal basis, which seemed more sensible, but I could not believe this had to be by spade and shovel for I had read of machines being used in Ireland. No, machines were useless with Falkland Islands peat. They had been tried and did not work.

The Fuel Officer allots a peat bog of about 150 yards to each householder. The bogs on the outskirts of Stanley are becoming exhausted. New ones are further away and increased distance adds to the transport cost. At the beginning of spring, that is in September or October, a householder marks out several yards on the top layer of his bog after estimating how much he will require for a year's supply of fuel. Then he starts to cut sods with a spade, each one being the size of a brick. He reckons to finish this part of the task by December. Then comes the rickling, exposing them to air on all sides so that they will dry thoroughly and shrink. This takes a few weeks. Being in the open does not matter for the wind is very drying and after a heavy shower the streets did not remain wet for long. Finally, the peat sods are carted home by lorry and carried in empty paraffin drums to the large peat shed, a feature of every house, and inside the shed they are stacked in heaps ready for use.

Apparently early settlers like the Chelsea Pensioners did this in exactly the same way, only they used horse-drawn or hand-carts instead of motor lorries, but it did seem to me dreadful that nothing quicker could be devised in an age when machines can do nearly everything. I was shocked at the appalling waste of man-power. In a back number of the *Falkland Islands Monthly Review*, I came across a suggestion that an overhead monorail system, as was in operation in Morayshire Scotland, be used for conveying rickled peat from bog to firm ground where lorries could wait to be loaded without sinking. As it is, a man wheels it in a barrow. That had never been taken up. Then I came across a book published in 1909, and found that four years previously the Governor sent samples of Falkland peat to England and a report was issued after examination by experts.

"As it seemed likely that this peat would yield a compressed fuel of good quality, full information regarding modern methods of compressing and bricquetting peat was supplied to the Governor, and as a result proposals have been received from a South American syndicate to work the deposits with a view to producing compressed peat fuel for consumers in the islands and on the South American mainland."

Nobody I asked had heard of this. Presumably the report lay buried in the Secretariat archives or been burnt in one of the disastrous fires that destroyed hundreds of documents. The archive-room, to which I was given access by permission of the Colonial Secretary, was still in a chaotic state where papers and files rescued from the last fire were stored, but there was no spare staff to sort them. As for the peat-cutting, one person said if it were not for that Kelpers would not know how to occupy their spare time. Another hinted that it was good for them. I expected him to add that Satan found mischief for idle hands! I felt like quoting from the Sermon on the Mount, "Consider the lilies of the field . . . they toil not, neither do they spin. And yet . . . Solomon in all his glory was not arrayed like one of these." I know hard work is inevitable in a harsh climate, that peat is the only cheap available fuel and it must be got out of the ground or people would die of cold, but after seeing Kelpers toiling away in the peat bogs like helots I was thankful I lived in a country where one could be a lily of the field.

Peat can be used for central heating, though not as a rule with small-bore pipes, but in Stanley the usual custom is to have a peat fire burning in the sitting-room and a Rayburn in the kitchen for cooking and water-heating. Rayburns were very satisfactory with peat. I had read Eleanor Pettingill's book on the Falklands written after her visit in 1953, and she suffered as only an American can from cold rooms and lack of hot water. That was not my experience sixteen years later. Both in Stanley

and the Camp it was warm indoors and there was always lashings of hot water for baths.

But peat is a dirty dusty fuel, and the British women hated
it. One told me, "I've cooked with charcoal over a brazier in
Khartoum. I've used coal and gas and electricity in England.
Now I've come to the Falklands and it is this ruddy peat. Well,
I only need to try atomic energy and I shall have sampled cook-
ing with the lot."

Housewives had plenty of labour-saving devices, such as
washing machines, cleaners, and mixers, but they still clung to
old-fashioned habits like shaking mats or beating them in the
garden. I was told this was necessary because of the peat dust
that got into everything, so also was frequent washing of
curtains and covers. Shopping and preparation of meals was
more difficult than in Britain because of the limited range of
foodstuffs. Most homes have deep freezers, and often refrigera-
tors as well, but to buy frozen food like vegetables and poultry
is expensive. Fresh meat was only 7d. a pound in Stanley. It was
very poor mutton, and even poorer beef. Sheep were kept for
their wool, not primarily for consumption, although there were
exceptions; I have had delicious mutton when entertained by
farm managers and ex-managers, but speaking generally, it was
lacking in flavour.

Outside every house is a huge meat safe, for the butcher does
not deliver less than half a carcass and the housewife herself
has to chop it up. When a joint is finished with at table the
remains are often flung on the garden so that the bones will
act as fertilizer, and as plenty of meat is left clinging to them,
it is a common sight to see gulls and domestic fowls pecking
together, so mutton even helps with egg production. Of course
helpings of meat are enormous, four chops per person being
considered normal. I heard of one shepherd in the Camp who
ate for his breakfast every morning twelve mutton chops, six
penguin eggs, plus tea, toast and marmalade. Pigs are not kept
on the Falklands and all ham and bacon is imported from
Britain. In fact, apart from a little beef, meat diet is synonymous
with mutton. It could easily be varied by upland goose—which
is delicious and very plentiful—an occasional home-reared
chicken and fish; but Kelpers do not care much for fish, and they
are not enthusiastic about fishing in such dangerous seas where

sudden storms may arise. In recent years, angling has become a sport, at any rate for men from Britain, who go to one of the few island rivers, the Malo, not so far from Stanley. This has been stocked with brown trout *(Salmo fario)* and a kind of cod, called mullet but bearing no resemblance to the red or grey mullet we can buy.

Cattle are merely kept for local needs, and on the Camp, where plenty of pasturage exists, there is a profusion of milk, home-made butter and cream. The picture is different in Stanley. As there are no roads even across East Falkland, surplus from the Camp cannot be brought into town, and the pasturage nearby can only support a dozen cows, whose milk has to suffice for 1,000 inhabitants. The cows are T.T., but I never felt happy about the bottling of milk in old gin and whisky bottles. I did not see how they could be so effectually sterilized as the thick glass ones used in Britain. The answer would be cartons, but they would be expensive to import. As for the butter situation in Stanley, that seems to me ludicrous. It is all imported New Zealand butter, but instead of coming direct from the country of origin, it goes all the way to Britain first, then a consignment comes back to the Falklands in the A.E.S., having done 16,000 miles more than necessary. No, the butter boats passing the Falklands would charge £1,000 to stop. Could they not fling out a load and have it picked up by a waiting boat? I asked, remembering a mail drop from a ship I was on as we passed the Canaries. Apparently that would not be practical either.

Fresh fruit, tinned fruit, jam and marmalade are also imported from Britain. Kelpers do make jam from the berries of diddle dee, and it is very nice, while they preserve rhubarb that, strangely enough, grows abundantly, even in Stanley. Willie May showed me a piece that was 4 feet long and weighed 2 pounds, and Heather often stewed some, which I did appreciate for I felt the lack of fresh fruit acutely. It is very expensive to buy. The Newest Store put out a statement that each apple cost the management 1s., and as people would not pay the price they were not going to import any more. Mr. Desmond Peck, owner of the Philomel Stores, made a special journey to Montevideo to purchase a large consignment of fresh fruit, so, when a notice came over the Box that it would be on sale at four o'clock that afternoon, I joined the queue outside the Philomel. I spent £1 on six oranges (at 1s. 0½d. each), six bananas and ten apples. Mr. Peck kindly threw into my bag two extra bananas as a present, and I felt mean when I refused to buy one of his queer-looking cucumbers, which were short, very fat and yellow. The potatoes were red, and of course expensive because they could not be grown in Stanley. It did seem absurd they had to come 1,000 miles when there were plenty in the Camp.

Although neither Falkland Islanders nor British residents entertain much owing to lack of domestic help, I was invited to a few lunches, afternoon teas and dinner parties. Being aware of the catering and staff difficulties, I realized how skilful my hostesses were in producing such excellent food. I shall always remember with gratitude the kindness of certain Stanley folk and the hospitality I received from them. Then, as a visitor, I was officially entertained by the Governor and his wife, and the Colonial Secretary and his wife. I also went to a few big town parties sometimes given to raise money for charity, but found these very dull with the same curry suppers, the curry too mild for my taste and lacking many of the usual ingredients. At such parties, large quantities of drink were consumed. The Falkland Islands have always had the reputation for hard drinking; this habit is partly because of the severe climate, and partly, I suspect, because of boredom. People have so little to interest them. True there were social clubs. I never went to one, as women were only admitted in the Colony Club once a week and had to be introduced by a male member, while the Falkland Club, known as the Gluepot, was exclusively for Kelpers. Sports clubs did not interest me. I was invited to speak once at the Women's Corona Society, but could not be asked to join as I was not the wife of a government official or there in a government position. Then there are charitable organizations which raise a great deal of money, mostly for world causes, such as relief in Biafra, for there is no poverty in the Falklands. The Anglicans, Catholics and Nonconformists all have annual bazaars. I went to the Roman Catholic one that was held during my stay and which realized the staggering amount of £1,700.

I went once to the weekly film show held at the Town Hall. It was not really enjoyable. I do not care for Westerns, and the news feature was a Carribean tour by the Queen that, judging by the out-of-date fashions, had taken place a few years ago.

The Stanley Dramatic Society, founded in 1964, produced a play, and I had the honour of being invited by the Governor to join a private party he was taking, after dinner first at Government House. Another event was the South American Evening that was held during the Archdeacon's visit. The Anglican Bishop and the Archdeacon live in Buenos Aires, the centre of the diocese which covers much of Latin America as well as the Falklands. But such is the anti-Argentine feeling that many Kelpers boycotted this function as 'thin end of the wedge', whereas it dealt with missionary activities in many countries.

The Stanley town library had a comprehensive collection of books on the Falklands and Antarctica, and, although the bulk of the lending department's stock was not very up-to-date, I found plenty of books I was glad to borrow—ones I had not previously read, also old favourites to re-read. The librarian, Miss Madge Biggs was very helpful and interested in my own work. She claimed descent from one of the original Chelsea Pensioners, longed to visit England but had only been as far as Montevideo. I hope now there is chance of her wish being granted.

Stanley is a strangely quiet town when the wind drops, as it does now and then. I have walked along the streets late on a summer evening and been struck by stillness that was so intense one could feel it. Even during the day there was not much noise of traffic. Dogs did not bark. Birds did not sing or chirp.

The most beautiful bird I saw in Stanley was the red-breasted troupial, also known as the military starling, and quite wrongly called the robin by Kelpers. It was the size of a starling and the male had a brilliant rose-pink breast. The southern black-backed gull, or Dominican gull, was everywhere, pecking at sheep bones in gardens, sitting on peat-shed roofs, or scavenging in the harbour and pursued by skuas. I loved the cumbersome logger, or steamer duck, which is unable to fly because its wings are so small in proportion to its body. Once I watched a logger with five ducklings. She approached a sewer pipe and spread her wings out—not to fly which she could not do, but to assist her to scramble on top of the pipe. Her family knew they were expected to follow Mamma, but were not quite sure how to tackle this obstacle. One duckling swam further out and climbed up the pipe where it was lower in the water. Another was more ambitious. He tried to get up the part where his mother was, fell backwards into the water, emerged, then decided his brother's route was safer. The rest of the family agreed with him.

Surf Bay, a good place to see birds, was 3 miles from Stanley, and the first time I set out to walk there, along a miserable stony track, I heard a Land-Rover rumbling behind me. Once level, it stopped and I saw driver and passenger were girls in the B.A.S. office. They offered me a lift, explaining they were going to burn office papers at Surf Bay. The only alternative was to make a bonfire on the corporation rubbish dump and they hated that place. "Besides, this gives us an excuse to get to the sea for an hour," said the driver.

We bumped along the winding pot-holed stony path, and, as I was nearest the left-hand window, I had a spectacular view of Stanley's inner harbour and The Narrows. Turning back was a panorama of hills, including the striking peaks, the Twin Sisters. Suddenly we stopped. The girls had cameras and decided to take photographs of cows eating kelp, or seaweed, beside the shore. Great strings of this kelp, like horrible twisted snakes, lie on sand and rocks and in the water, and I wondered at the cows liking it, but I suppose grass was poor and scanty. One of the girls said she heard kelp gave the milk a salty flavour.

Another few minutes and then we came to an even more abrupt halt, for on the narrow pebbly beach was a solitary king penguin. This species has but recently returned to the Falklands to breed, and the only breeding ground is much farther from Stanley so this one must have strayed here by accident, possibly looking for a mate. He was 3 feet high, with the usual penguin white-shirt front, a blackish-blue back and head, but he had a bright yellow beak and striking yellow patches round his eyes. It was the first time I had seen a penguin except in zoos and, as I instinctively take an anthropomorphic view of mammals and birds, I began regarding him as a sedate old man wearing a dinner jacket, a non-scientific reaction to penguins which is deplored by serious naturalists. Then I saw he was a vain and alert penguin and that he was glancing at the three of us with an obvious desire to impress. I loved the way the orange around his eyes extended down his neck when one studied him closely and how the vivid colouring merged into the snow-white of his glossy breast. He glowed in the sunlight. He advanced a few feet forward, flapping his flippers, then stretching his neck, then preening his feathers. He did not in the least mind us standing a few feet away with cameras pointed at him. No royal personage could have been more obliging in permitting his photograph to be taken.

We dragged ourselves away with great reluctance and drove on to Surf Bay. The wide sweep of sand was so white that I thought at first snow had been falling. As for the sea, never have I seen such a heavenly shade of green. It only became blue far in the distance. For the whole sweep of the bay it was the colour of malachite—not aquamarine, for it had not the faintest suspicion of a blueish tinge near the shore. Inland the pearly sand merged into hills, white at first, then brown as they became covered with diddle dee. I saw a hare racing up one, and he did go fast.

I had come without field glasses but did not need them for the birds let one come quite close, though not so close as I could to the king penguin. There were plovers, dotterells, logger ducks, upland geese and a couple of black oyster catchers. The male oyster-catcher was pursuing the female, and she was alternately giving him the brush-off, then encouraging him.

On the way back we stopped to look at a dead turkey buzzard. One of the girls said it had been shot. "And a good thing too," she added. "They destroy lambs." Close by she pointed out a quark, or night heron, a bird only found on the Falklands. It has very dark-blue plumage streaked with green, and from the back of its head streams a grey and white feather, about 3 inches long, flowing out like a pennant. The next time I saw a quark was on a solitary island called Trieste. That was during an inter-coastal trip I took in November. Then in the New Year I paid a return visit to Weddell Island and a visit to Carcass Island, and in both islands quarks were nesting in trees near the manager's house. Normally no trees are available and they nest on the ground, so it is curious that instinct leads them to a tree whenever such a rarity occurs on the Falklands.

The girls dropped me at Glasgow Road and I thanked them over and over again for giving me such a delightful morning. This was the last day of October, late spring, and a mild sunny day with a temperature of 60 degrees, that was high for the

Falklands. There were nice days, there were days when there was no wind, but what I did find trying about the weather was its unpredictability. One never knew what clothes to wear, and was therefore either too cold or too hot. If it was warm in a morning, there would be a sudden drop in temperature of several degrees. Still, the Falklands have a healthy climate with very fresh, almost intoxicating, air. I never experienced insomnia while on the Falklands, so I can certainly recommend their therapeutic value in cases of sleeplessness.

5

A Week on Weddell Island

A FEW days after my arrival at Stanley I settled down to examine the file of letters from the B.A.S. office, and discovered that as far back as February Mr. Clapp had written to a dozen sheep farms. As a matter-of-fact, the number was more like twenty, but I never saw all the replies and felt very awkward two and a half months later when I found I had been expected to stay at two I did not know about. In the file were twelve letters and copy of the one sent by Mr. Clapp. He said that a Miss Taylor, an authoress, was coming to write a book on the Falklands and that B.A.S. was asking the manager to give me every facility when I came to his farm. To support my *bona fides*, there was a statement to the effect that the Colonial Secretary knew and approved of my visit.

My writing plans had certainly been broadcast over the islands so it was a good thing I had not tried to shelter under an alibi like Mary Kingsley did. As it was, Mr. Clapp's circular letter must have worried some managers who wrote back asking what facilities I required when I came and what I wanted to do. One man said he must make it clear that I was expected to pay my own fare from Stanley to his settlement. I should think so! Another asked to be sent a list of the books I had already had published. Another, to my horror, was expecting me in August, a couple of months ago, and had made arrangements for my accommodation.

Before I could answer these letters, with apologies for not having done so earlier. I had to decide if it would be possible to visit all the farms, or make a selection. My host, Willie May, explained about the Beaver air service and what it cost. The Assistant Colonial Secretary, Mr. Bound, had already booked for me on an inter-coastal voyage of the *Darwin* in the New Year, and that would include calls at some of these settlements, but both Mr. Bound and Mr. Clapp were ill with influenza so I could not consult them. I discovered too that it was going to be difficult to find someone who knew the Camp as a whole, not just a few farms. Falklanders only travel for pleasure to Britain and to Uruguay. Stanley people with relations in Camp may visit them, although usually the reverse happens, and there are many, many folk in Stanley who have never been into the Camp. Britishers are the same. It seemed incredible to me that men should come for two or three years to a far-away, little-known place, like the Falklands, yet neither they nor their wives bother to see any part of the islands except Stanley and its immediate surroundings.

I turned back to the file of letters, weeded out the farms that I should see on the *Darwin* trip and concentrated on the others. A letter from the manager of Weddell Island, a Mr. Ferguson, was very welcoming. On the map I saw Weddell was a fair-sized island lying between West Falkland and New Island. Anyway, dipping into the hat, so to speak, I decided to take Mr. and Mrs. Ferguson's invitation as acceptance number one.

This is a disgression, but I ran into trouble when posting my first four replies. The wind was blowing with gale force when Willie May drove me to the Town Hall to get some books from the library. A pillar box was near where he parked and I fought my way to it. It was very foolish of me to be so careless but being buffeted about by the elements had made me stupefied, so as I started to put the letters into the box the wind caught the last and whipped it out of my hand. I chased it in vain over the road and into the grounds of St. Mary's Roman Catholic Church, where it vanished. Unfortunately I had no idea which of the four letters it was and I quailed at the thought of writing four explanations to four unknown sheep farm managers. In the end I rang up the Postmaster whom I had met at the new Colonial Secretary's house. He said he would have the contents of the pillar box brought to him next morning so that he could check which of the letters I had written were there. He rang me to say he found letters addressed to Darwin, Chartres and Port Howard, but nothing for Weddell. I wrote again to Bob

E

Ferguson. He never got the first one, which must have ended up in the sea.

Willie May's stepfather, Peter Anderson, lent me a large scale map of Weddell and the adjacent islands, all owned by John Hamilton Ltd. Some of the names were delightful, such as Pudding Mountain, Hell's Kitchen and Useless Bay. Mount Weddell, 1,256 feet high, lay close to the settlement, and marked near it was one of the stone runs that I was anxious to see. Heather had once flown over Weddell, returning in the Beaver after a visit to her old home on West Point Island, and the pilot told her to look for the guanacos on Staats Island, part of the Weddell group. There was also a curious rock in the sea, shaped like a horse and called Horse Block. Willie, too, knew about the guanacos. The late John Hamilton experimented in bringing over creatures from South America to see if they would establish themselves in a different environment. Skunks, rheas, bandarios (a type of golden ibis) and Cape Horn otters all died, but guanacos and Patagonian long-haired foxes survived; the foxes proved a menace to sheep and now efforts were being made to exterminate them. Hamilton also crossed ordinary ponies with Shetland and produced an animal about the size of a Welsh cob.

Later, after I returned from Weddell, I met the firm's overseer, Mr. Robertson, who told me a good deal about the development of sheep farming on that and the adjoining islands, also about John Hamilton's early struggles. The Weddell group and Saunders Island in the north-west, are now owned by his son-in-law, Señor Gallie, who lives in Argentina and has a huge estancia there.

Weddell Island covers about 100 square miles, roughly the size of an English county. It used to be called Swan Island, and the name survives in a headland, Swan Point, but during the first half of the nineteenth century it was renamed after Captain James Weddell, a sealer and antarctic explorer, who lived from 1787 to 1834. He is also commemorated by the Weddell Sea, Antarctica. From the 1770s onwards Weddell was a base for provisioning and sheltering from storms ships of whale hunters, many of them from North America. They did not settle, only used it as a temporary haven. Sheep farming was begun by the first owner, a man called Williams, who came to the Falklands in the F.I.C.'s early days and whose daughter married their Colonial Manager, F. E. Cobb. Williams also had two sons, and the younger one, Major Williams, sold Weddell to John Hamilton in 1921.

Hamilton was born in Thurso, a town in the extreme north of Scotland. He emigrated to the Falklands as a shepherd in 1880, and in ten years he managed to save £80 out of his meagre wages. Then he left for Patagonia, hoping to start his own farm, but first he tried to buy sheep from the F.I.C., who refused to sell him any, thinking that a shepherd receiving £5 a month from them, and now giving up that wage, would never be able to repay his debt. Undaunted, Hamilton secured land at Punta Loyola, near Gallegos, and—with three companions, men named Fraser, Kyle and Saunders—went hundreds of miles northwards to find cheap sheep. Driving the flock back to Punta Loyola nearly all the sheep died, and, though his companions left him, Hamilton worked and saved the money to buy more. The same thing happened again, but his third attempt succeeded and he began to farm on his own, growing richer and richer. In 1921 he paid a return visit to the Falklands and bought Weddell and Beaver and other small islands close by. In 1940 he came again and purchased Saunders Island, named, not after his former companion, but after Sir Charles Saunders, First Lord of the Admiralty in 1766. Stories are still told of Hamilton's meanness even after becoming a millionaire. On one of his visits to Stanley he brought his wife. She was wearing the first fur coat she had ever had and he kept telling everyone how much he had paid for it.

I booked to go to Weddell by Beaver on 30th October, but I was soon to discover that on the Falklands nothing could be depended upon to happen as one planned. For some days before the wind was blowing with gale force. There were messages on the R.T. like this, "Dr. Gallimore can't get away from West Point. He is windbound there." Of course the Beavers could not fly, and a backlog of flights was built up, with the result that I did not fly for another four days. It was a lovely calm morning when the Air Office rang me to say I was listed for the second flight and would I please be at the hangar at a quarter to ten.

When I arrived at that dreary shed, minus waiting-room or

any of the amenities one expects with air travel, there were several people, not all passengers, and two pilots and two mechanics. A passenger for the second plane was a girl returning to Speedwell Island, and I got into conversation with her and the friend seeing her off. On learning my destination, this friend said Mrs. Ferguson of Weddell Island came from South Wales, a place called TreThomas near Caerphilly, and I knew at once we should have a lot in common for I lived in the same county and had often been to Caerphilly. Travelling by the first plane were the Pole-Evanses of Port Howard, just returned from a long vacation in Britain, whom I had met in Stanley the evening before. We had a mutual friend, Dr. John of the National Museum of Wales. Now they were being seen off by two Stanley friends, a retired F.I.C. Colonial Manager and his wife.

No payment was required until return, so there was no issue or collecting of tickets, only baggage weighing. The pilots did the weighing, and one joked with Mr. Pole-Evans about the large amount he and his family had and threatened extra charges. They all laughed and Mr. Pole-Evans got on the scale himself, I think to demonstrate loss of weight since his holiday. The pilot merely raised my case a few inches off the ground and pronounced it O.K. without any further worry. The Speedwell Island girl also satisfied him with hers. A young man with ciné-camera had none.

We three, scheduled for the second plane, stood just inside the hangar, opening to the sea, and watched the Pole-Evanses scrambling into what did indeed look a toy kite. Their luggage was tossed in after them, pilot climbed aboard, and two mechanics wearing waders pushed the little Beaver into the water. Then they detached the wheels on which she had gone down the slope and she began drifting on her floats. The engine was started and she soared into the air after a short skim along the sea. Next came the turn of the second plane. The man with the camera sat by the pilot. I learnt he was one of the 1968–9 hovercraft unit and was making this 'tourist trip' before he sailed for Britain, so as to take pictures of the scenery. In the row of three seats behind sat myself and the Speedwell Island girl. I noticed safety belts were provided and that she was fastening hers, so I did the same.

One of the B.A.S.-owned ships, the *John Biscoe*, had been away for several months, undergoing repairs at Southampton. She was just arriving back at Stanley and approaching the public jetty as we took off, and to celebrate her return we made a detour, circling overhead with everyone waving before we resumed course for the first touch-down at Fitzroy settlement. Fitzroy is about 10 miles away and it is one of the F.I.C. farms. As the Beaver only rose 1,000 feet above ground, no higher, I had a splendid view of the treeless undulating land below, with its carpet of light green grass broken by diddle dee and other growth, and by the shining lumps of quartz that appeared frequently and impressed upon me the ruthless nature of the Falklands where land as well as sea is a challenge to man.

At Fitzroy we landed in the harbour. All around the islands are creeks, bays, and long inlets, the latter affording especially good harbourage. From the plane, as she came to rest on her floats, I had my first glimpse of a typical settlement—the few white houses with red roofs, the dominating 'Big House', the cookhouse, the shearing sheds, and fenced pastures where cows, horses, and sheep were grazing. A small jetty jutted out from land, but we were some distance away and a rowing boat came to collect mail and parcels. There were no fresh passengers.

After leaving Fitzroy we flew over the sea, still at only 1,000 feet up, and I could see the kelp or seaweed that grows so thickly round the Falkland coasts. It lay in mile-long strands on top of the water, like a congregation of giant sea serpents, and now and then a bunched-up mass of golden growth shone brightly and was less horrible than the wavy strands. Now we were over Lively Island, but instead of landing, the pilot turned the plane sideways and we tilted so much that I was thankful of the safety belt to keep me steady in my seat. He swooped down, causing commotion among sheep and geese and hens, who ran about in all directions, while a few human beings emerged from houses and waved. The pilot opened the window nearest to him, letting in an awful blast of air, and flung out a mail bag. Then he shut the window, turned the plane back to normal horizontal position, and we were off again.

Mail drop was part of the Beaver's duties, but in strong wind it may have complications. Once a bag dropped at Port San Carlos was blown away and only discovered two years later. Another time, on Carcass Island, the bag stuck in a gorse hedge and the owner, Mr. Bertrand, and a shepherd were hunting everywhere, not having seen where it had fallen, so the pilot had to hover around until he could show them its position.

We dropped mail at three more places—Bleaker Island, Sea Lions Island, and North Arm on East Falkland, but Jim Kerr, the pilot, circled Sea Lions and flew low and slowly over a sandy beach where dozens of these creatures lay basking in sunshine. The plane did not perturb them. I saw sea lions closely on further Camp trips. They are not seals, though often commonly called so by Kelpers. Two species of seal, the southern elephant and the southern fur, do breed on the Falklands, but not in large numbers and in places now designated as sanctuaries. The elephant seal breeds on the Twins, off Carcass Island, and the fur seal rookery is near one of the Jasons.

When the hovercraft man had got the shots he wanted, we made for North Arm, then Speedwell Island, where we came down to leave the girl passenger, and the jetty looked as if everyone had come to welcome her. Now we were crossing Falkland Sound, the channel that separates the two large islands, East and West Falkland, and our rate of progress slowed down considerably. I gazed at the lovely blue sea, shimmering in the sunlight, but though there were no waves, only gentle little white crests of foam, it had the sinister kelp spoiling its peace. There was something so macabre about the kelp. I hated the stuff. To be caught in its strands means death. I was glad for my thoughts to be interrupted by Jim Kerr producing a flask of coffee that he shared with me and the hovercraft man, the latter being busy all the time with his ciné. The noise of the engine made conversation impossible, though Jim Kerr shouted out place names he saw I was trying to identify on my map and he pointed to the 100-foot-high screes coming down sheer to the sea on the eastern coast of West Falkland. Later, he drew my attention to the Arch Islands, like their name, and, as we came into Port Stephens, to a set of rocks on top of a hill that were known as the Indian Village because of their resemblance to wigwams.

Port Stevens received its name as early as 1766, being called after Sir Philip Stephens an Admiralty secretary. It is the largest of the F.I.C. farms, having an acreage of 182,800. Although this was the first time I saw it, the place had very sad associations, for here, a few days after arrival, Sid Barnes, whom I met on the A.E.S., had had a fatal accident. Roz, his widow, returned to England the same time as I did, but at present she was still in Stanley. They had invited me to come to Port Stephens and stay with them after Christmas, and, but for this tragedy, I thought how happy they would have been in their new venture. I had heard so much about their plans on the voyage out that it seemed a bitter mockery to be looking at Port Stephens settlement and not seeing them there.

We were up against the jetty and one passenger came aboard. Next stop would be Weddell Island, and that was not far away, so Jim Kerr told me. Very soon we were skimming down on the blue waters of the harbour in front of that settlement. Like Fitzroy and the others there were a few houses and other buildings, and there were lots of gorse hedges in full bloom, the gold gleaming against the green of the pasture land, while in the distance was the impressive crag-topped Mount Weddell. People were waiting on the jetty but Jim Kerr came down several yards away and said he could not get any nearer, so a boat was rowed to collect me, my suitcase, parcels and mail. Very soon I was ashore and being greeted by Bob and Thelma Ferguson, then introduced to a woman called Betty, two men, Davy and George, and two small children, a girl and a boy. The girl was Teena Ferguson, who, as we walked along, told me she would be 7 in a fortnight and that she had a brother John, aged 9, and he was away at the Darwin boarding-school.

The cookhouse was quite near and there Bob Ferguson sorted the mail for himself and the others. Weddell is a small settlement, there being only the manager, the foreman, five shepherds and a sixth on Beaver Island, cowman, and cook for the cookhouse where the bachelor shepherds live. It was another five minutes walk to the Ferguson's home and we had smoko as soon as we arrived. Smoko is an Australian term for the mid-morning break, tea, not coffee, always being served. I thought privately that a quarter past twelve was late for this and wondered when we should have dinner, then I realized I ought to have put back my watch an hour. Stanley has summer time but not the Camp, a confusing arrangement that involves switching backwards and forwards as one travels from one to the other. The Camp says an artificial change of time upsets the farm routine while Stanley likes the extra hour of light for peat cutting.

Two extensions had been put on the 'Big House' at Weddell, but it was far smaller than the majority of managers' houses I saw, later, and less modern. The original part must have been built towards the end of the previous century, probably for the first owner, Williams, and it consisted of small hall out of which opened a sitting-room and out of that a kitchen, while from the hall a narrow spiral staircase led to two attic bedrooms with sloping roofs. At a later date a very large dining-room was added on the other side of the hall. After that came the second extension which consisted of an extra kitchen built on to the old one, now a living-room and very cosy with its Rayburn. The new kitchen was equipped with modern sink and cupboard units, but as the floor was on a lower level Thelma Ferguson had the perpetual inconvenience of going up and down three steps. Leading out of the new kitchen was a big larder. Then, as part of this extension, a door from the living room led to a passage, and off this were bathroom, two bedrooms and office. This section was centrally heated by an old-fashioned boiler in an outhouse. When Thelma first came, the cookhouse cook had been on Weddell for forty years and he said even the second extension was built before his time.

Thelma had the house very warm and comfortable, and she assured me there was plenty of hot water so that I could have a bath every night, but she warned me about one Camp inconvenience. Electric power is supplied by a generator and this only runs from sunset until an hour before midnight, so my bedroom light would automatically go out at eleven o'clock. Of course this means for the Camp housewife that washing machines and electric irons can only be used in the evenings, though often the generator is switched on specially for Monday mornings.

Dinner was a hearty meal with such a colossal helping of roast beef that I implored Bob to give me less. Then he wanted to pile potatoes and swede on my plate. The second course was tinned fruit and fresh cream, the cream being put on the table in a two-pint jug, and Thelma was quite shocked at what she considered the small amount I took. Over another cup of tea my entertainment for the afternoon was planned.

So far the only penguin I had seen was the solitary king penguin on my way to Surf Bay. I was delighted to learn that there were several rookeries of gentoos quite near the settlement, and Teena was only too happy to be my guide. We set off immediately after dinner, walking through the paddocks, but I noticed how careful this small 6-year-old girl was to shut every gate that she opened. After the paddocks we came to moorland, and after several minutes we turned right, in the direction of the sea. "There are the penguins," said Teena pointing for ahead, and soon I could distinguish the colony.

The gentoo *(Pygoscelis papua)* is widely distributed through antarctic and sub-antarctic zones and is the only species of penguin to have conspicuous white marks on its head. He has a vivid reddish-orange beak, orange feet with black claws, a bluish-black back, a black head with white band from eye to eye, and the usual white shirt front. Like all penguins, he shuffles or waddles on legs that are far more use to him in the water where they act as rudders, and because of this they are placed at the rear of the body. Only on land does any penguin adopt the upright position that makes him look like a comical gnome.

The colony, which was one of four, had about 100 gentoos with nests that were merely shallow round holes scratched in the bare ground. There was no grass left on the entire site, just dark brown slimy earth stinking from the birds' dung. Each nest was only 3 feet away from the next, and over the majority stood or crouched a penguin, whose white breast shone as glossily as if polished but was often streaked with blood and dirt. Gentoos are quarrelsome creatures and frequently scrapping. These nesting birds were females, who had just laid, or would soon be laying, their regulation two eggs. Lined up on grass outside the perimeter of nests, the 'housing estate', was an assembly of males, apparently doing nothing but surveying the scene. Once chicks began to hatch they would be busy, either fetching fish from the sea to feed their offspring, or letting mothers do this while they guarded the nests. Exposed eggs could be left—in fact, that afternoon many females were taking a break from the tedious business of hatching—but a gull or skua would soon seize an unprotected chick.

Penguins are usually very curious but these gentoos were not in the least interested in us, while, like other Falkland birds, they were not normally frightened of humans. I found I could crouch to take a photograph within a few feet and a gentoo remain perfectly indifferent. Still I was horrified to see Teena shooing some of the nesting birds off their eggs, then chasing them in their retreat to the line of husbands. I called Teena and she obediently came running back, but the column of spectators was now in panic. Dozens of penguins were scurrying up the small hill, the more nervous ones falling on their stomachs and propelling themselves over the ground more rapidly than by waddling in an upright position. Some even used their flippers to increase their speed. All of a sudden confidence was restored. Like a column of soldiers in response to a captain's command, the gentoos turned round and returned to their original position, except for the females who came back to nest duty, but without undue haste. Even then, while making your way to 'Chez Nous', or 'The Haven', it is amusing to pick a few quarrels with neighbours *en route*.

I was so intent on watching these bickerings that I did not at first notice the mischievous Teena. She was swopping eggs by putting different ones in different nests. However this did not upset the gentoo mothers in the least. Once one had concluded her quarrels and identified her own nest, she settled down with a loud contented squawk and proceeded to incubate two eggs she had not laid. So that Teena should not continue her teasing—and she thought it just good fun—I asked her to collect diddle dee for I noticed some of the birds smartened up their miserable nests with bits of diddle dee and grass. Teena was delighted with the idea and while she was away I watched a gentoo, who so far had not laid an egg, stealing decorations from a neighbour who had left her nest to take a stroll. The thief worked hard so when Teena returned with her hands full, I restocked the robbed nest, then guarded it until the owner appeared. This gentoo pecked and pulled a little at the oddments, but did not appear to realize they were new additions to her home, nor that the original decorations had vanished. She settled down, after giving raucous expression to her contentment, while Mrs. Thief on the next nest looked sublimely innocent of any stealing.

I could have stayed far longer watching the gentoos, and I did pay two more visits to the rookery while I was on Weddell, but Teena was impatient to show me the shearing sheds and other settlement buildings so we walked back over the moor, she making sure I avoided any patches of bog. Grazing cows were pointed out to me and a couple of horses patted for my benefit. We climbed an occasional fence but mostly used the gates, all of which she carefully shut and latched. I soon realized she was making a detour to show me the sheep dip and shearing sheds, and once inside the latter no detail was omitted. Outside, three sheepdogs who had joined us were patiently waiting, and when we came out they greeted us boisterously and escorted us home.

After supper Bob Ferguson talked to me about the farm and Weddell Island. On Sunday he and Thelma planned to take me to Loop Head where I should probably see the Patagonian foxes. I enquired about stone runs and found there were several around Mount Weddell, one within easy walking distance. Teena was to show it to me next day.

Like everyone else, when I saw this unexplained phenomenon I was very impressed. Huge boulders of quartz rock lay jumbled together in a 'stream' or 'river' that meandered along for more than a mile and spread out in 'tributaries'. Width varied from a few feet to several yards. Mostly the boulders were white or whitish-grey, but lichen and fern occasionally had a foothold, showing up yellow and dark green. According to Charles Darwin, if you bend down over boulders devoid of vegetation you can hear the trickle of water, but though I did this I never heard any such sound. Rivers petrified by angry gods, was the description that came into my mind as I wandered around Mount Weddell stone runs.

The time I spent on Weddell Island was fascinating and most enjoyable, while I could not have had kinder hosts than Bob and Thelma. With Thelma coming from a part of South Wales that I knew well, we became friends immediately. We drank endless cups of tea and we talked and talked, mostly about Wales and her family in Caerphilly. She first met Bob in Southampton, and when they married he tried to settle down in Glamorgan, but she could see he yearned for the Falklands so they came out, spent some time in Stanley, and had now been a few years on Weddell Island. I asked Thelma did she not find the isolation hard to endure? Well, she admitted it was trying at first, but she had grown used to it. She was very interested in the farm. It was a healthy life for the children. And in another two years, Bob would be due for six months leave so they could visit her family in Wales.

Weddell was a small settlement and its social life democratic. On the other side of the island was a shepherd and his family living at Kelp Creek, while the shepherd—unmarried—on Beaver Island did indeed lead a solitary hermitlike existence, but apparently he liked it. He gave orders for stores over the R.T., and every three months Bob sailed there in the schooner to deliver them and inspect the sheep. This shepherd was a man in his fifties, a clever carpenter and a first-class cook. He made jam for himself from diddle dee and rhubard. Recently Bob went to Beaver with one of the marines stationed on the Falklands and they were served with a mouth-watering fruit tart.

Like all Camp wives, even those married to managers of large farms, Thelma had to work hard. Because there was a cowman she was spared the task of milking, but she had to make bread and churn butter, as well as do the ordinary household chores, without any help. She also helped Bob with his paper work— and a manager has a lot of this to do—and with him ran the Camp stores; she also supervised Teena's homework.

Camp education leaves much to be desired, but the difficulties created by tiny scattered groups of children and by roadless islands, are almost insuperable. The present Superintendent of Education, Mr. Draycott, has done a great deal to improve the quantity and the quality of education, but he is far from being complacent about the situation and sadly laments shortcomings that he cannot remedy. Except at Port Howard (and a few other settlements), where there is a full-time school with schoolmaster, teaching is carried out by itinerant teachers who visit the settlements in turn, holding classes for a week and leaving the children with homework until the next visit. On Weddell, John Ferguson was at boarding school in Darwin and the family of one shepherd were under school age, so the travelling teacher had only two pupils, Teena and a boy who was also 6, David. Richard, whose full name I never learnt, came every three weeks, his time being divided between Weddell and Port Stephens and New Island. Teena told me the date he was next expected. "Richard sleeps at the cookhouse while he is here, but he gives

David and me lessons in the schoolhouse. You must come and see it. There is a Rayburn and it is lit the day before Richard gets here." Thelma saw that Teena did the set homework, but many Camp mothers are not so sensible. The system is a poor substitute for regular full-time teaching, only nothing better can be arranged under the circumstances.

I was very ignorant of sheep farming, even the seasonal routine of lamb marking, gathering, shearing, pressing and dipping, until I went to Weddell. Gathering and shearing start in the middle of November, provided weather is suitable, and they continue until well into February. By that time dipping will have started. Although Weddell and its adjacent islands did not constitute a large farm by Falkland Islands standards, yet to cover all that terrain entailed travel overland on horseback and sailing to islands like Beaver in a schooner. Beaver alone had a shepherd, but most of the small islands had sheep put on them for grazing purposes. Then in winter, shepherding involved continual care, or the loss of stock might be serious. As it was, the Patagonian long-haired foxes introduced by Hamilton had reduced the number of sheep from 10,000 to 7,000. This number was now rising through efforts to get rid of the pests. On our walks we often came across fox traps and Teena would demonstrate how they worked. For such a little girl she was remarkably well-informed on farm matters.

The first gathering of the season began two days after my arrival. Teena and I returned from a partial climb of Mount Weddell and found the stud paddock was crammed with sheep. Bob was hoping it would not rain or he should have to drive them into sheds for the night. Wet sheep cannot be shorn. The rain held off until mid-morning next day, and by then the 300 sheep were in the shearing sheds, and an excited Teena took me to see what was going on. I was shown the grading in different pens according to age, age being told by the animal's teeth. Ewes from five to six years were branded after shearing to show they were doomed to become mutton that season, but Bob explained that after a severe winter and backward spring, when loss among lambs was heavy, then ewes would not be slaughtered until they were seven or eight years.

Three men were shearing, two with electric clippers and one with hand scissors, the last being used on sheep coming along for the first time as cutting was not so close and they would be protected by the little growth that remained. I watched with fascination as a shepherd opened the door of a pen, bundled out a sheep, and held her against the left knee with the left arm keeping her steady as with his right hand he manipulated the clipping machine. It removed a fleece in four minutes. First the man loosened the underneath part, then the head, holding each ear to cut round it, then the legs, and lastly the back. He finished by pulling the detached fleece over the animal's head as if he were removing a petticoat. Occasionally a sheep might kick with hind legs, but most of them lay back against the shepherd's arm like pet teddy bears and wearing goofy expressions that showed enjoyment of the process. Once the fleece was removed from an animal, she was bundled into a pen on the other side where the shorn sheep were being assembled.

Davy Phillips, the foreman, picked up each fleece and carried it to a rolling table where he spread it out, twisted one end, rolled it into a bundle and, having graded it A, or B, or C, he tossed it into the appropriate bin. When visiting another farm I learnt that there may be sub-grades like AA, and, as London buyers must be assured a bale so labelled will contain only fleeces of that grade, it is necessary for one man to do this work, or else judgement might vary.

During the smoko break, Bob showed me his sharpening machine and a specially designed clipper, the latter being driven by a battery so that he could take it when he went to Beaver because there was no electricity there. After smoko I watched him counting the number of sheep shorn for the official record he kept. They should then have been put outside in pens to get used to being in the open without their fleeces, but there was such a bad squall of rain that they had to be kept under cover or many might catch pneumonia.

Next day the weather was dreadful. Although this was the equivalent of our early May, Mount Weddell and the surrounding hills were covered with snow, and last night's temperature had been below freezing point. Teena kept watch from the living-room window, reporting if she saw a sheep falling down with cramp due to cold, for Bob could not keep the flock penned any longer. The following day was not so bad, and it was cheering to know that no sheep had died. Certainly those in the paddocks looked less unhappy than they had twenty-four hours before. In the evening Bob showed me a catalogue of wool auction sales at the London Wool Exchange in Spitalfields. It was interesting to read about the different Falkland settlements and the amount they sent. Bob was very pleased with a letter he received commenting on the improvement in the quality of wool sent from Weddell and that it now had "speciality character". He still had fifty sheep to be shorn from this first gathering, and they would be done next day. On Sunday he would be free and hoped the weather would be fine enough for the expedition to Loop Head.

Time on Weddell simply flew. There was always something fresh to see and Teena, who had completely taken charge of me, was a delightful guide, whether showing me penguins and fox traps, or schoolhouse and stores, the latter being the nearest thing to a shop in the settlement. It was only opened on Saturday afternoons by Bob, while Thelma managed a separate room for clothing. The stores contained groceries, sweets, tobacco and alcoholic drinks. Money is not used in the Camp. Wages of employees are paid straight into their Stanley banking accounts, and against such an account is debited individual expenditure chits that the manager issues. When a shepherd buys a packet of cigarettes, he does not pay for them but signs a chit for the amount. The system seems to works all right, especially as the habit of saving a large proportion of wages towards a holiday in England or 'Monte' is strongly ingrained in the Kelper. The great disadvantage of it is that Camp children grow up without any understanding of money until they visit Stanley. Certainly they are taught about it in arithmetic lessons, but their experience is academic not practical.

Teena was very proud of the garden and was most anxious for me to take a coloured photograph of some stunted narcissi. Later, she told me, there would be lupins and snapdragons, "and we have tea out on Xmas Day because it is so hot then". Falkland conception of a heat wave is not ours. I was impressed by the large vegetable garden that was enclosed by a very high hedge of macrocarpa, 15 feet high, I should say. This had been planted and tended years ago so that by now it effectively protected the garden against the searing winds that made it possible for plenty of really good vegetables to be produced. One morning Teena took me to the hen house, where she collected eggs, and on the way home found a goose egg under a gorse hedge. This she carried in great triumph to show her mother and unfortunately dropped it on the floor and wept in great distress when it broke. Thelma kept a bowl of goose eggs in the larder, and a still bigger bowl of penguin. She wanted me to try a penguin egg, but I simply could not face one. However hard it is boiled the white is still an opaque jelly. Of course there were always at least two bowls of cream in that larder. Thelma had four bucketfuls of milk every day. So had Betty, one of the shepherd's wives, whose boy David was the same age as Teena so they played together as well as having lessons from Richard. Betty had lived in Stanley for some time, working at a dairy there, but after marriage she had been on New Island, at Port Stephens, and now Weddell. She had a pleasant house that was more modern in structure than the Ferguson's and when I had tea there a lovable ginger cat sat on my knee. Everywhere I went in the Camp, whether on East or West Falkland, there was always home-made chocolate cake for tea, a sandwich type with a thick mass of fresh cream between the two sections.

Sunday morning was fine but windy, and at breakfast Thelma told me Bob had eaten his and gone to fetch the lorry to take us to the Loop, although he was uncertain about weather and afraid the ground would be boggy. "But we'll go," she declared. It was 9th November, two days before Armistice Day, and Teena and David came to offer me poppies sent from Stanley the year before, and of course they were puzzled when I gave them money in exchange. In the end Thelma took charge of the coin because she was going to send a 'chit' to the Stanley Red Cross, for the Poppy Fund. They ran off to the cookhouse and over yet another cup of tea, Thelma and I listened to the R.T. Retired farm managers in Stanley were talking to their sons, now managers, and the wives were giving news of domestic happenings. I found it all most amusing and very jolly. Of course there is no privacy with the R.T., and no one expects there to be.

It began to drizzle, but we set off about half-past ten in the lorry, with Thelma, and myself cosily squashed in front with Bob. Teena sat on my lap. There was supposed to be a rough track for the entire $7\frac{1}{2}$ miles to Loop Head Hut, but Bob could

Weddell Island: *(above)* gentoo penguins and *(below)* a stone run

The Hill Cove 'forest'

Kidney Island, nature reserve. Above the beach is a maze of the tussac grass that covers most of the island

not keep to it much because it was so boggy and we bounced over rough ground, over hillocks of diddle dee, and crossed a couple of small streams by means of rickety bridges. At least they looked rickety with their supporting posts of half-decayed wood, but they bore our weight all right. It was wild desolate country and the land became quite narrow so that we could see the sea on each side, and lovely stretches of white beach. Bob pointed out the Harbour Islands which were covered with tussac grass and where he had put bullocks to fatten themselves prior to being killed. Two upland geese flew overhead. Then I saw some dottrells, then an unpleasant sight—two dead lambs that had been the prey of foxes. As I previously noticed on the Falklands, pieces of rock were always pushing their way through the thin covering of earth and grass, and as we got further on, these became more frequent and, in one part, formed a long ridge where the pieces of quartz lay in horizontal, not vertical, strata. The effect was primeval, frighteningly so, as if one had travelled back millions of years in time.

Near Loop Head was a shepherd's hut. Now and then some-one came to stay for a week, shepherding, snaring foxes or cutting peat, for the bogs used for fuel were concentrated in this part. It only took a week for a man to cut the settlement's annual supply—that is, working full time and overtime. The rain was intense when we arrived at the hut, and we rushed straight inside to shelter. The journey of 7½ miles had taken longer than an hour.

Bob lit a fire in the old-fashioned Stanley No. 9 range, that was used throughout the Camp until more modern stoves were introduced. He filled a colossal iron kettle and put it to boil. Meanwhile Thelma was unpacking eggs, bread, butter and tin of meat. She spread her delicious home-made butter on her home-made bread and cut slice after slice, while Bob opened the tin and put on the eggs. My usual guide, Teena, showed me round while we were waiting. The living-room-cum-kitchen was about 8 feet square. The floor was covered with rough mats made from sacking. There was a table, five chairs, and a dresser on which were set out Tilly lamp, candlestick and an assortment of crockery and cutlery. A door led to the bedroom, where there were six bunks.

As the meat was cold Thelma thought we ought to eat the

F

hard-boiled eggs cold, and they were easily cooled by Bob taking them outside and exposing them to rain and wind for a few minutes. The second course was one of her lovely chocolate cream-filled sponges, and we drank cup after cup of tea. The weather showed no signs of improvement. We cleared up and waited until two o'clock, Bob still hoping to go right to the headland but as no fox would appear in such violent rain, the homeward trek began.

Bump, bounce, sway, wobble, and by now I was used to swinging from side to side or bobbing up and down, as the lorry skirted bog after bog. Then I saw Bob had driven right away from sight of the broken, half-obliterated track, and we were ascending a hill and steering in a different direction.

"We're going by States Cove," explained Thelma, and Bob added that into that flowed Tern Hill Stream "that comes from the waterfall you were trying to find". I had seen waterfall marked on the map but failed to locate it.

The lorry was now on a crazy course that apart from speed was unrivalled by any switchback railway in a fun fair, worse because every fresh obstacle, either ascending a hill or going down it, was impossible to anticipate. As we lurched and jolted in descent, I realized we were making for a stream, or so-called river, and assumed we should cross this and somehow struggle up the other side, that is unless the lorry turned over and we were thrown out. I was really scared by now, but consoled myself by reflecting that Bob must be attempting something he knew to be safe as he would hardly risk the lives of his wife and child. Then we stopped. I said, "I thought you were going to cross the river," a remark greeted with much laughter. Thelma said, "Bob is hoping to catch a fish for our supper."

He put on waders and went down to the stream followed by Thelma and Teena, who waited on the bank. I remained in the cab of the lorry, and watched the proceedings, being soon joined by Teena who announced she was cold. Bob saw a fish almost at once, but it was elusive to catch by hand and he spent a long time, wading backwards and forwards as he groped under rocks to flush it out. His hands must have got terribly cold in the icy water. At last he caught a 3-pound 'mullet' and hurled it ashore where Thelma tried to kill it until he joined her and finished the business. Then we bumped and bounced back to the track, finally getting home at half-past five. By now the sun was shining and the gorse hedges brilliantly golden. It was bad luck that all day the weather should have been so unkind, but though I had not seen a Patagonian long-haired fox, I had had a memorable day.

After a fish supper I talked to Bob about the various animals and birds from South America that John Hamilton tried to establish locally. Only foxes and guanacos remain, and the guanacos are also a menace to the sheep industry because they avidly consume tussac needed for sheep. Tussac is a tough grass growing about 5 or 6 feet high, forming great balls around the roots on top of which are stems and long hanging leaves. Due to lack of foresight by past generations of farmers, it has vanished from many parts of the Falklands. Staats Island, where Hamilton put the guanacos, was covered with it. Ten years later it had all disappeared and though 1,000 roots were planted in 1933, there is no tussac there now and the guanacos feed on diddle dee, and soon that will have vanished, with consequent soil erosion.

The guanaco is a pretty elegant creature with graceful neck and a yellow and brown coat. He is a close relation of the llama, but smaller. I found a reference to them also having been put on Sedge and Split Islands, only could not discover if this was so, or if any were still there. Bob Ferguson just talked about them on Staats, and in the *Falkland Islands Monthly Review* for February 1959, I read about two men, by arrangement with the then manager of Weddell, going there for a week and shooting-off 111. Bob said they were difficult creatures to shoot but something would have to be done about them as they were rapidly multiplying.

6

Back to Stanley

THE morning of my departure from Weddell was sunny and windless. I had said good-bye to Bob the night before, as he would be getting up at 6 a.m. to go sheep gathering on horseback. Over my late breakfast I listened to the R.T. My name was on the flight, and 'Edith' gave an approximate time, adding that the previous port of call would ring Thelma as soon as the plane left for there was no radio on that Beaver. The call came. Then Thelma, Teena, and I strolled to the cookhouse from where we could see the plane alighting in the harbour.

I left Weddell about half-past eleven, thinking we should fly direct to Stanley but, as I had already discovered in the Falklands, nothing happened as I expected, and this flight turned into a tour that lasted five hours. There was only one other passenger, a young man who sat in front with the pilot.

I soon heard that we were calling at Sea Lions Island to pick up Dr. Ashmore, the senior Medical Officer of Health. "I left Doc. on the way," shouted Jim Kerr. "He'd got to give an injection to the baby there." On the way out we dropped mail and skimmed over Sea Lions, but this time we came down, landing on a huge pond quite near the sea and like an enclosed harbour. From the plane I could see a high bank covered with the fantastically-shaped tussac, the long grass blades hanging down gracefully from high pedestals formed from tangled growth, and between the plant roots were paths of sandy soil. At the end of one, watching the plane, was a jackass penguin. This species is not the true jackass penguin, but the Magellan (*Spheniscus magellanicus*), and the only penguin that nests by burrowing into the ground. It is smaller than the gentoo, its sombre black colouring relieved by a broad stripe of white that extends along the sides of crown and neck, while it has white underparts. Although scientifically incorrect, I prefer to use the name 'jackass' by which this kind of penguin is known all over the Falklands.

Only the owner and his family live on Sea Lions Island, it being one of the few farms belonging to a single individual. Companies own the majority; including the F.I.C. which has farms on both East and West Falkland, its total holdings comprising 46 per cent of the total available land. Other owners may have one partner, possibly a retired manager, living in Stanley, with his son as present manager. This is the case with Chartres which is owned by Anson and Luxton. Then there are non-resident landlords, like the Gallies of Weddell and Saunders Islands, who live in Argentina but have an overseer in Stanley, Mr. C. Robertson.

With the addition of Dr. Ashmore we flew from Sea Lions to Goose Green, its population of 100 people making it the biggest settlement while it is reputed to have the largest shearing sheds in the world. Adjacent, and really part of Goose Green, is Darwin, where stands the 'Big House' and a boarding school for Camp children that was built by the F.I.C.

Dr. Ashmore had to see several patients and was driven away in a Land-Rover. Jim Kerr told us two remaining passengers that we should have to wait at least an hour and a half for the doctor so we could not stay in the plane. We climbed up a ladder to the jetty and Jim left us to have dinner with some friends. Stranded like this, the young man and I walked slowly past the huge shearing sheds, empty and closed, and past houses with shut doors. There was not a sign of life anywhere, not even a dog barking. Apparently everyone was at home eating a midday meal, so Goose Green looked like a village of the dead, a plague-stricken spot where one could imagine crosses being painted on the doors with "Lord have mercy upon us" underneath. In this depressing atmosphere my companion started to confide his woes and I soon found he was a Very Angry Young Man. His was a story I heard again from others with similar experiences, and substantially the facts were the same.

My Angry Young Man had come from England a year ago under a four-year contract as shepherd on one of the sheep farms. Part of his grievance was that he had been thoroughly misled over conditions by the person in England who interviewed him. For one thing, he was told that a Land-Rover supplied by the farm manager would take him to Stanley every Saturday night so that he could go to a dance there. From his farm the Land-Rover would have had to cross Falkland Sound, the 20-mile sea channel between East and West Falkland! Later I met another victim of this propaganda, but though he went to a farm on East Falkland, the same island as Stanley, he speedily discovered that it would take him seven hours in good weather, more often ten, to get across the intervening stretch of roadless terrain, that is if he did not get stuck in a peat bog. Of course no manager would supply shepherds with means of transport for such a journey.

Other fairy stories included being wakened with hot coffee and biscuits every morning by the cook in the cookhouse, so he need not take an alarm clock. Well, my Angry Young Man had reached such a pitch of disillusionment that, during his manager's absence, he had got on the plane and he said he should not go back. Yes, he would have to refund £80 for breaking his contract—perhaps more—but there were still savings from his wages banked in Stanley that he could claim, and he would get some kind of a job until he had a passage on a ship for returning to England. He did not care. "They" could put him in gaol, but he was not going back to that farm.

When I had an interview with Mr. Goss, Secretary of the Falkland Islands General Employees Union, I told him about this meeting. He agreed that only too often men came from the United Kingdom badly briefed, but when he tried to help them he found that they had not troubled to read their contract properly. If they had done so before signing, then clauses in that— and it was in standard form—would have cleared up many misapprehensions. Still, from other complaints I heard later, especially about farm conditions, I do not see how these could have been explained in any contract.

Then men used to conditions in Britain find the feudal state of society on some farms—though only on some—unbelievable. They cannot accept a boss who has the power of a Victorian squire. They consider inhabitants of the 'Big House' a lot of snobs. One man raged against having had to call the manager's children Master and Miss. Of course a visitor like myself could not assess the situation fairly, and it did not arise on small settlements like Weddell. When I visited bigger ones, I could see that the manager must maintain discipline over workers, some of them ignorant of Falkland sheep farming, while I should think that it might make discipline difficult if his wife and children became too intimate with families of shepherds and others. Naturally all must be friendly for even the largest settlement is a community on its own.

But the men who come and soon break their contracts must be a wasteful nuisance to managers. Dissatisfied employees are uneconomical. Obviously some should never have been passed by whoever interviewed them in Britain, as ability to give a different way of life a fair trial is an obvious qualification. I heard of one who only stayed forty-eight hours on the farm, then returned to Stanley. My Angry Young Man seemed to think he could get a job there easily, and actually he did until he sailed, but I met another of his kind who said he had been unable to do so. He was told he must first obtain a work permit. When he went to the office that issued them, he was told he could not have one because there were no jobs available. In the end he went as shepherd to another farm until he got a passage back to England, and he said he had to pay back £115 for breaking his contract.

I got very tired walking round the deserted Goose Green and listening to the Angry Young Man's tale of disillusionment, so at last I said I was going to knock at the next door and ask if we could go inside and sit down until the plane was ready to leave. My choice was a fortunate one. The owner immediately invited us in, gave us tea and the inevitable chocolate cake. We chatted and I found I had met his father who was in charge of the Globe Stores at Stanley. This is the oldest shop in the town and dates back to 1863.

When we left Goose Green we had two extra passengers. One was Mr. Draycott, Superintendent of Education, who had been visiting the Darwin School, and the other was Mr. Vinson, manager of the settlement. He had business at Lively Island and got off there. Then we flew to Fitzroy for Dr. Ashmore to see patients. We passengers stayed with the pilot in the Beaver, but the doctor was so long that Jim Kerr grew impatient and after revving up his engine and making a terrific noise, he took off, pretending that he was leaving. We circled the harbour, came down again by the jetty to see a Land-Rover tearing along with an alarmed Dr. Ashmore rushing out as soon as it stopped. He laughingly shook his fist at Jim as he scrambled into the plane.

We arrived at Stanley at five o'clock, four hours later than I expected, but I had seen a jackass penguin and I had heard the story of an Angry Young Man. Learning over the R.T. the time of my return, Heather had got Willie to come and meet me so he was waiting inside the hangar as the mechanics waded into the water, fixed wheels under the Beaver, and we were towed up the causeway by a jeep. I did appreciate Willie coming with transport—and the Mays were very kind to me in that way as well as in others—for Stanley had no taxis, so without a friend one would be helpless and just have to walk, however much luggage one had.

Heather was excited because the first cruise ship of the season was due to anchor at Port William the next morning. She was too big to come through The Narrows but passengers would come ashore in launches always provided the weather was suitable. The year before it had been too windy and none could come, a great financial loss to Stanley shopkeepers who found sale of china penguins and other souvenirs (all made in England) very profitable. I went out immediately after breakfast and found the Newest Store full of goods that I had never seen displayed before. In and outside shops and other buildings were notices "Keep The Falklands British", and Union Jacks were hung all over the town. We heard all the passengers on the Kungsholm were Americans, and I thought that they could not have any doubt about the Falkland Islands belonging to Britain, but strange to say some did.

Early in the afternoon Heather and I could see from her windows that the ship was lying at Port William, and Heather went out to be at the public jetty when the first launch arrived. I stayed in to write a letter of thanks to Thelma Ferguson and was later about to go and post it, and get a view of the tourists, when Willie appeared with a couple he had met, a Mr. and Mrs. Jack De Vries of Tusan, California. They were delighted to be invited inside a private house and went into raptures over Heather's choice of furnishings, also the air of comfort. Of course the peat fire interested them. Over a cup of tea Willie explained how peat was obtained and promised to drive them to a bog in his vehicle. We talked about Argentina's claim to the islands, and they told us about the cruise that had started from San Francisco, went down the west coast of Latin America, calling at Lima, Santiago and Punta Arenas. From Stanley they would visit Buenos Aires, Rio and Barbados, ending up at New York. Willie took them to see a peat bog and, though they were longing to see penguins, the nearest likely place was too far for the time at their disposal, but he took them in the Newest Store to buy souvenirs. I was with them and the shop was packed with Americans, not only spending money on china penguins and ash trays ornamented with Falkland Island maps and crests, but on clothes and rugs and cases to hold their purchases. Heather joined us, and finally we took Mr. and Mrs. De Vries to the jetty to catch the half-past-five launch.

Four days later the second cruise ship came. She was the *Hanseatic* and though her passengers were again naturalized Americans, a large number were second generation Germans, Italians and Spanish, and still spoke the tongues of their fathers. This time, it was arranged for those who wanted to see penguins —and nearly all did—to be taken for short trips as far as places like Volunteer Point and Sea Lions Island by the two Beavers; and a number of Land-Rovers were commissioned to take parties to York Bay, often a haunt of penguins but not a place where they nested. The overland trip was not very successful because the Americans did not like being bounced and shaken along the rough track that led to the bay, and the penguins swam off after a few parties had arrived. The Red Cross provided teas, and a story went round that the Governor's wife, who was helping, went to invite some stray tourists inside and when asked what her husband did for a living, she replied, "Oh he is here on a four-year-contract job." Even better was the story of a party gate-crashing into the grounds of Government House, where they came across His Excellency gardening, and mistaking him for the gardener they asked all sort of questions about "this governor whom we were told represents your British Queen", and was he anywhere about? Others visited the "most southerly cathedral in the world" where the senior chaplain and his wife conducted them round, while tourists keen on stamps thronged the post office. Going into the Newest Store next morning, I heard that shopping had been even busier than on the 14th. One tourist bought ten shirts and another two identical pairs of shoes, while ladies' sweaters and slacks and skirts were in great demand, such goods being much cheaper than in the U.S.A. The ridiculous china penguins, stamped underneath "Made in England" were so popular that there was not one left in Stanley, and Mr. Peck of Philomel Stores told me he was hastily cabling an order to London for a stock of 2,000 to be sent out on the next A.E.S., hoping they would arrive in time for the January cruise ships.

Incidentally I went to the Air Service office to pay my return fare of £15 10s. to Weddell Island. I had only received the bill that day, and the office would not take it without the bill. They did trust one on the Falklands!

I mentioned seeing the wreck of the *Great Britain* as she lay derelict in Sparrow Cove when coming into Stanley in the A.E.S. I would have liked to be taken by launch to go over her, but there was no chance of that. However, I did have an opportunity of seeing one of the old wrecks scattered about Stanley harbour. The Manager of the Newest Store, Mr. Elwyn Owen, offered to take me over the *Charles Cooper*, which was used by the F.I.C. as a storehouse, but retained much of her original character, including some beautiful carving along her transom. Of course I was delighted to accept Elwyn's invitation, although I felt rather jittery when he took me into his office and asked me to sign a statement in which I promised I would not hold the F.I.C. responsible if I had an accident.

There were two hulks together, the *Actaeon* and the *Charles Cooper*, and quite near the shore, but we had to row a short distance. The beach was strewn with pebbles, broken glass and mussels, in what seemed to me equal proportions, and as Elwyn rowed along the blades of his oars became covered with snaky coils of kelp. He went very slowly around the *Charles Cooper* for me to see the exquisite carving. In a pamphlet, *Condemned at Stanley*, John Smith gives a full description of the three shields and the drapery and foliage surrounding them. He says that this transom stern "must surely have been one of the best examples of the wood carvers' craft" when the ship was built, which was in 1856. She came into Stanley harbour on 25th September 1866, and her estimate for the repairs she needed was so costly that her owners sold her for a store hulk. There were many other such cases, which accounts for the many wrecks in and around Stanley, the port being a centre for repairing work between 1850 and 1890 when wooden ships sailed round Cape Horn on their way to Australia.

When we had had a good look at the carving and taken photographs, Elwyn wedged the boat against the *Actaeon*, which lay embedded in mud and was covered with horrible slippery green slime, and I pulled myself on the rotten timbers that had once been her deck. From this ran a jetty made of steel yards, taken, I was told, from another wreck, the *Fennia*, now at San Francisco, where she is being restored prior to becoming a show relic of the sailing ship era. This led to the *Charles Cooper*.

She was very large for a wooden ship of her time—850 tons. I saw that the bridge deck was covered with aluminium roofing to keep the F.I.C. stores dry, and that windows were built into the sides. While I was looking round, Elwyn and I were joined by the expert, John Smith, who showed me where the cabin passengers' saloon and cabins used to be, also where the captain and crew quarters lay in the bows. Then he pulled up a loose floorboard for me to look down on the lower deck where the unfortunate steerage passengers endured the voyage. We walked along to where the anchor was pulled up, and before we left he pointed out the thickness of the wooden beams, while three layers of wooden 'walls' made the sides 2 feet thick.

It was a unique opportunity for seeing over a genuine old wreck, the kind of opportunity that one could only get in Stanley, and utterly different from seeing a wreck restored and refurbished as a showpiece for the public. Presumably this will ultimately be the fate of the *Charles Cooper*, for she has been bought from the F.I.C. by the South Street Seaport Museum of New York, and will be taken, as John Smith puts it, "to recreate in the heart of the City the old seaport of New York" when she is placed among other 'old-timers' in this museum.

One of the 'musts' for me while in Stanley was a visit to the local museum, now in very cramped inadequate premises in a small room in the town hall. The old town hall, library and museum were destroyed by fire in 1944. During the last few years, Mr. Thompson, the Colonial Secretary who had recently left, did his utmost to amass fresh material and, although the objects were badly displayed and overcrowded in their present home, I thought he really had done a wonderful job considering that so much of value had perished.

Among the cases was a geological one containing bits of iron ore and iron deposits from Mount Usborne, also some curious stalagmitic formations. There were relics from ships; a figurehead from a barque *Garland*; and three books from the library of the *Allen Gardiner*, a ship connected with missionary work in Patagonia and with a mission station on Keppel Island in the Falklands. Commander Gardiner, born in 1794, had the idea of a Falkland mission station preparing a few selected Fuegians for work among their own people in Tierra del Fuego, and Keppel was a training centre until 1898 when it became just a farm. I was particularly interested in the *Great Britain* relics case, which had a copy of the builder's model of the ship. There were natural history exhibits, photographs, charts and the Argentinian flag that was planted on the Stanley racecourse by the Condor members in 1964. It is a great pity that better premises cannot be found for this museum and a temporary trained curator be appointed to reorganize display of existing material and systematically collect more, for there must be plenty of interesting objects lying around in Camp houses.

Apart from Keppel Island, religious history of the Falklands is centred in Stanley, and principally concerned with the Cathedral. The first bishop, Bishop Stirling, was consecrated in Westminster Abbey on 21st December 1869, and took the title, Falkland Islands. At first he was only responsible for the islands and for a mission on Tierra del Fuegia, but in 1874 consular chaplaincies in South America were put under him. Now the diocese covers the whole eastern part of that continent, including Argentina, and both Bishop and Archdeacon reside in Buenos Aires, while a senior chaplain lives at the Deanery in Stanley and is in charge. The cathedral, designed by Sir Arthur Blomfield and consecrated in 1892, is a handsome brick-and-stone structure with a tower whose clock has a face on each of the four sides. The two other churches on the islands are also in Stanley—St. Mary's (Roman Catholic) and the Tabernacle (United Free Church).

Falkland Islands stamps are in great demand by philatelists, and this, I suspect, accounts for the popularity of pen pals there. I heard of one girl at Port Stephens who had seventy. The *Falkland Islands Monthly Review* often contains requests like, Mr. So-and-So of New York "would like to correspond with a view to exchange of stamps"; or, somebody else explains he "is a schoolteacher and interested in the exchange of F.I.'s postage stamps and First Day Covers". In the August 1969 *Review* I read about the revenue received from a commemorative stamp issue of the twenty-first anniversary of the Government Air Service and how it brought £3,424 5s. 10d. into the Government's coffers. It was inevitable that the centenary of the first Bishop's consecration—that of Bishop Stirling—should be observed in stamp form as well as in other ways, and a date late in 1969 was fixed for the appearance of first-day covers.

In order to secure a portion of the revenue obtained for church funds, the senior chaplain agreed to be responsible for stamps being put on these covers, thus relieving post office staff of the extra work. He organized parties of voluntary helpers. I joined and spent several afternoons at the Deanery, where Jill, Peter Millam's wife, directed us, worked herself and kept us going with cups of tea, currant bread-and-butter and cake. When the two Deanery children, Rosalind and Kevin, came home from school they made themselves useful by handing round food and re-wetting the pads on which we moistened the stamps. Jill Millam was very kind to me in many ways. In fact I owe a great debt to Peter and her for their help and ready hospitality. Apart from coming to stamp-working parties and morning coffee parties, I was welcomed at the Deanery at any hour I chose to call. It was a real 'home' where I could chat freely, even grumble about things that perplexed me on the islands. Peter's mother was a Kelper, though he was born and brought up in England, as was his wife, but the islands had always attracted him so when there was a vacancy for senior chaplain, he tried for the position and, as was the custom, accepted a four-year contract. This would expire in another six months, and Peter told me that when he left the Falklands he would feel he was leaving behind a part of himself. There is a magnetism about them that does attract those of Kelper birth and those of Kelper, or part Kelper, descent.

But for the company I should soon have become bored with the work of sticking four stamps (2d., 6d., 1s. and 2s.) on each first-day cover, and they had to be carefully and exactly affixed. The other helpers were both Kelpers and temporary British residents, some of the latter daring to be amusingly frank about Stanley's shortcomings. I remember one relating some suggestions she had been making at the Colony Club to the wife of a high-up colonial official for improving arrangements for the reception of cruise-ship tourists.

"What these Americans want is to see penguins, and to take photographs of themselves with penguins. It is no use a few Land-Rovers running folk out to Rookery Bay and finding the stray penguins there have flown away. The Government should arrange for a dozen penguins to be caught the day before from Kidney Island or Volunteer Point, put in cages, and kept until the tourists leave. Twenty-four hours of that wouldn't hurt the birds, and the Americans would be thrilled. Then there should be penguin eggs on sale. Why not? There are plenty. And why can't Government House be opened like a stately home, with an admittance charge, of course, and the Governor's uniform on show in a glass case? Think how these visitors would love his white plumed hat. Well,"—and she mentioned the lady's name —"was quite interested, and she said, 'You've got a point. I shall tell my husband.' But Mr. —— was listening, and I'm sure he disapproved of my ideas."

Chatting to a Kelper who has been brought up on Camp, I asked her about the isolation, but she said, "Oh, I enjoy being alone for hours except for birds and sheep. I prefer it to town bustle and noise. When we go on leave to England, we get away from London the first minute we can and take a cottage in Devonshire and avoid even village life." A wife of a retired sheep farm manager agreed she felt the same, but the rest working round the Deanery dining-table knew nothing about the Camp, had not been there, and most of them had no desire to go. My tastes are urban as regards a permanent home, and I should hate isolation for any length of time, but I had found Weddell Island so enjoyable that I was eager to see more of the Camp and decided I could not wait until 30th December before going there again.

I called at the F.I.C. offices for a list of *Darwin* pre-Christmas sailings and found, after her arrival in Stanley from Montevideo on 18th November, she was due to sail in another couple of days for the settlements of Fitzroy, Goose Green, North Arm and Fox Bay. I had already seen the two first places, but not the other two, and they were not on the itinerary of the 30th December trip. I was particularly interested in a visit to North Arm because the shepherdesses from Britain were there.

The appeal for shepherdesses to come to the Falklands had been issued a year ago, and it received a good deal of publicity, newspapers having articles with such titles as "Girls queue for Bachelor Islands". After saying that there were eleven bachelors for every spinster, one writer added that not only girls in search of husbands wanted to go to the Falkland Islands, but many with experience of tending sheep. I saw a photograph of one successful applicant, and underneath it said that three other girls were sailing with her. Travelling out on the A.E.S., we brought the pet sheepdog belonging to one. Then, at a Deanery stamp-sticking session, I heard how one of our helpers met the girls arriving from Montevideo by the *Darwin* and with two hours to spare in Stanley before being flown by Beaver to North Arm.

"They hadn't a clue about the place. They had been told they could go to dances every Saturday night in Stanley. 'My dears,' I said, 'You've a hope! How could you get here from North Arm?' One said, 'But aren't there buses that can bring us?' 'Buses, but there are no roads! No, there isn't a bus on the Falklands, and not likely to be.' That upset them, and one asked if she could get to the mink farm while they were waiting for the plane—hoping, I suppose, to buy a mink coat on the cheap— but I had to disappoint her about that when I explained the mink farm had failed and been closed for a few years. 'Look here, my dears,' I said, 'You'd better do some shopping while you've got the chance.' 'But aren't there shops in this place where we are going?' Poor girls! I wonder how they are getting on?"

I wondered too as I booked my passage in the F.I.C. office.

7

More Sheep, Sea Lions and Penguins

I **WOKE** during the early hours of 18th November to hear the wind howling, and when I got up for breakfast I saw the ground was white with snow. Certainly it vanished during the morning, but it was disappointing weather for late spring and if I had not been so keen on this second Camp trip, I think I should have rung up the F.I.C. and cancelled.

In spite of strong winds, the *Darwin* had not been delayed in coming from Montevideo. She had just arrived at the Company's jetty, and waiting to come to the public jetty was the B.A.S. ship *John Biscoe*. Though not an ice-breaker, the plates of the *Biscoe* are strong enough to cope with ice, and the dark brick-red paint on her hulk and funnel make her easily visible under antarctic conditions. By contrast, the *Darwin* has a great deal of white paint on her deck structure; but she does not go to polar waters. I was curious to get aboard and compare her with the A.E.S. According to the scheduled list she should leave for Camp on the 20th, but on the 19th, a phone message came from the F.I.C. office to say she was sailing at half-past seven that evening, and passengers must be on board by seven. Heather made me tea and sandwiches at half-past five because she was afraid the sailing time was too late for an evening meal to be served. She was right. I was very grateful, both for the high tea and to have the extra sandwiches she insisted on my taking. Willie drove me to the jetty. I had a double cabin to myself, and on looking at the list of passengers I found there were only two others—a Mrs. Morrison and Paul Charman, the Minister of the Tabernacle.

The wind had dropped, and from a shelter on deck I watched us glide through The Narrows into the outer harbour, and I saw the Pembroke lighthouse and the notorious Billy rocks on

Kidney Island: *(above)* the tussac grass and *(below)* a rockhopper penguin with chick

West Falkland : typical bay leading to a settlement

A typical sheep farm station settlement

which many ships were wrecked in the days of sail. It began to get chilly. I went to look at the library case in the lounge and picked out a novel of C. P. Snow, although I knew I had read it before. A Uruguayan steward was in the bar so I ordered a drink and was sipping it when the Reverend Charman came and sat by me. Like Peter Millam he told me he was in the Falklands on a four-year contract, and now his congregation was paying for this trip in order that he might contact Camp Nonconformists. He asked me questions about the book he had heard I was writing, interested pertinent questions which I was delighted to answer.

I did wake next morning when we dropped anchor off Fitzroy, but it was 5.30 a.m.—in fact 4.30, because the clocks were an hour earlier to fit in with Camp time. Paul Charman had said he was getting up then to go ashore, but I was far too sleepy and, consoling myself with the excuse that I had been to Fitzroy before, I dozed off until the steward came in with tea and biscuits.

Paul and I were the only two at breakfast. Mrs. Morrison, the third passenger, travelled as far as this first port of call, and had now gone. We were due to leave at half-past nine and Paul said it would take four or five hours to reach Goose Green and Darwin. I spent the morning reading, with trips up to the deck but found it too cold and windy for sitting there. At lunch Paul and I were joined at our table set for three by the Mate, a Mr. Jones, who informed me that he was also connected with Alginate Industries and appointed by that company to act as liaison officer in negotiations between them and the Falkland Islands government. Later I learnt that Mr. Jones and his wife ran an *estancia* just outside Montevideo, and that she was a South American. As for Alginate Industries, I heard a good deal about them while I was in the Falklands—even before that, for, during the Lord Chalfont crisis, it was mentioned one evening in an I.T.V. news programme that a Scottish firm was interested in taking over Falkland Islands' seaweed and working up an industry.

I have spoken before how one sees this kelp everywhere around the coast, even in Stanley harbour, and how menacing and vicious it appears. Only the upper leaves and stalks are visible, and these trailing along the surface of the water show the direction of the current. Hidden below are stems so long that they stretch to the bottom, and roots, which may be as much as 12 feet in circumference, are attacked to rocks and large stones. But kelp is a useful commodity, rich in mineral salts, and it is farmed in various parts of the world, even grown artificially in some places for harvesting purposes. The Scottish firm referred to on television was Alginate Industries Ltd. and had for some time been considering setting up a plant on the Falklands. In the *Falkland Islands Monthly Review* for April 1969, it was stated that a representative was expected shortly to make arrangements for work to begin in another year and that a local office was already opened in Ross Road, Stanley. At the Stanley schools prize-giving I noticed the firm gave a prize for chemistry. Then in the 1970 January *Review*, a Mr. Gooch, the prospective engineer and Colonial Manager for Alginate in the Falklands, was said to be due to expedite matters. While it was hoped that the scheme would come to fruition, there was a good deal of scepticism, for Falklanders have seen so many attempts to establish industries other than sheep farming, but all so far have failed.

The *Darwin* reached Goose Green about a quarter to three in the afternoon, but had a difficult job to tie up at the jetty for the wind was now blowing at gale force. I saw one rope was secured to an ancient wretched-looking hulk lying beside the jetty, and the piece of wood with the rope split off and had to be retrieved by a small boat. I was waiting to go ashore when Mr. Jones came to tell me that it was too windy for the companionway but he thought I could manage to get over the ship's edge and jump down to the jetty, which, with assistance, I did. Then I struggled along the jetty, being nearly knocked down by the wind, but I got to a sheltered passage between two of the colossal shearing sheds, paused there for breath and was met by the manager, Mr. Vinson, who said his wife was expecting me for tea. Mr. Vinson explained that he first had to go on board and see Captain Miller, but could drive me to his house very shortly if I did not mind waiting a few minutes in his Land-Rover. I was only too thankful to do this and get out of the wind. Besides I had had enough of wandering about Goose Green with the Angry Young Man on my last visit there. It was quite interesting to sit in comfort and watch cargo being brought off the *Darwin*. There were also sheep being driven off a small launch moored by the jetty, and their instinct led them at once to grass. Without hesitation, they hurried along, looking neither to left or right, but off the jetty, between the sheds, along a track, to pasture land where they stopped and began to graze.

Mr. Vinson drove at what seemed to me a terrific speed over the mile of rough track that led to his house, which was in Darwin, where the settlement originally started. The route was a twisting one, and we crossed cattle grids from time to time; and, like Weddell, there were lovely hedges of gorse in bloom. We passed a huge round kraal, a perfect example of dry-stone walling, and he explained it had been built by gauchos to enclose cattle in pre-sheep-farming days. Then we came to the manager's house, and its front entrance was through a beautiful conservatory, full of geraniums and begonias. Mrs. Vinson came to greet me and took me into the sitting-room, a bright room with flower-patterned chinz covers on chairs and couch. I noticed the radiators for central heating and she told me this worked satisfactorily on peat fuel. There was a picturesque fire-grate but empty, and certainly no fire was needed in addition to the radiators, for the room was quite warm.

At tea we were joined by a Mr. Meade, one of the grassland officers, or, in local parlance, grassmen. A team of five agricultural advisers came from Britain in September to spend eight months examining all aspects of grassland and livestock farming in the Falklands, by the request of the Government. I had already met Mr. Williams at a dinner-party in Stanley. He was from the Veterinary Investigation Centre at Worcester. In addition there was a veterinary surgeon, a livestock specialist, a pasture specialist and this Mr Meade, who was an agronomist. Mrs. Vinson and Mr. Meade discussed education. She, I knew, took a great interest in the nearby Darwin boarding school for Camp children. Then the conversation drifted to the Welfare State and from that to problems of the Falkland Islands. Mr. Meade told me I could not really grasp Camp life until I had seen the utter isolation of some shepherds—like, I suppose, the one on Beaver Island, only Mr. Meade had not yet been to Weddell. We were all in agreement about the majority of Stanley people knowing nothing about the Camp. There was a section there who said the farms ought to be split into smallholdings, but Mr. Meade thought that was against the modern trend, at any rate in England, where expensive mechanization cannot be multiplied in a number of small farms, so the bigger one has it every time.

We were half-way through tea—tea with chocolate cake—when Mr. Vinson came in with a F.I.C. representative, a Mr. Gilmour. Goose Green and North Arm were, like Port Stephens, F.I.C. farms, and this gentleman was one of the high-ups in England who came to the Falklands every few years in the capacity of overseer. He was staying the night with the Vinsons, and next day he and Mr. Vinson were going to drive overland to North Arm, where they said they would be seeing me. Then I was driven back to the *Darwin*. She sailed at eight o'clock that night.

The ship was at North Arm when I came down to breakfast and Paul Charman had already gone ashore to begin his round of visits. I walked down the companionway about ten o'clock. Thank goodness I was not expected to use a rope ladder as on the A.E.S. On North Arm jetty I was met by the manager, Mr. Oliver, who took me round the sheds where shearing was just beginning. They were far bigger than the Weddell ones, but then Weddell had only 7,000 sheep, where as Mr. Oliver told me North Arm had 60,000, plus another 2,000 on an island called Bleaker. He took me over to the pressing machine and I saw how that was operated, then how the bales were made up —and I remembered this when I was on a wool-collecting trip in the New Year and every sheep-farm jetty was covered with the bales waiting to be loaded on to the *Darwin*. The sheep dip was interesting. Mr. Oliver explained that a sheep should not be in the dip more than one minute, and while it is the practice in England to plunge the animal in, North Arm has a 'run' through which the sheep has to swim to get out, and the swim takes exactly the requisite minute.

We drove past the collection of settlement houses, including a new £6,000 one built for the shepherdesses. Mr. Oliver gave a very good account of the girls. They had settled down very quickly and were good workers. They even insisted on taking their share of peat-cutting, which is not considered a woman's job. "But we want the same pay for it as the men get," they told him.

The Big House at North Arm was some distance away and

had only been built nine years ago, so was very comfortable and modern. There was the usual entrance porch, where grew fuchsias, snapdragons, geraniums and an orange tree that did not bear any fruit. Mrs. Oliver also showed me her tomato and melon plants. I thought the house very well planned and most attractive with its wide hall and curved staircase. All the bedrooms but one had beautiful views. The exception looked on a small cemetery, no longer in use, said Mrs. Oliver, as corpses were now flown to Stanley. When burials were done locally, the manager had to read the service, unless a minister could get out from Stanley, but usually there was not time for this.

The *Darwin* captain, Captain Miller, arrived and the four of us had smoko in the lounge. Mr. Vinson and Mr. Gilruth were also expected for lunch, but their overland journey from Goose Green might well be delayed through the Land-Rover sinking into a bog. I think Mrs. Oliver was worried about her dinner being spoilt so she was relieved when there was a telephone message from a shepherd, who lived in a distant cottage on the route, and he reported that he could see them coming over the brow of the hill.

Lunch was one of those superb meals which I so often had when being entertained in the Camp. We had delicious, properly under-done beef as I like it, roast potatoes, leeks and horse-radish sauce, followed by rhubarb crumble and quantities of fresh cream. This was concluded by coffee served in the lounge. Mrs. Oliver had no help in the house. She had done the entire preparation and cooking herself.

Captain Miller then left us to return to the ship after asking Mr. Oliver to get us three—myself, Mr. Vinson and Mr. Gilruth —there by four o'clock, the time he wanted to sail. We had an early tea and left in good time, but when we reached the jetty the loading was not finished and I was able to have another look round the shearing sheds with Mr. Oliver. He introduced me to one of the shepherdesses, a bright pleasant girl but too busy helping a man to fold fleeces to spare time to talk to me. When we were outside again I saw the one who owned Wendy, one of the sheepdogs travelling on the A.E.S. Wendy was never as friendly as the other dog, and now she refused to know me. Mr. Oliver introduced me to her mistress, but though this shepherdess was sitting on a lorry waiting to be joined by other workers then driven home, our conversation was rather short. She appeared satisfied and determined to stay the three and a half years to complete her contract.

Mr. Oliver talked about sheep and how they always go with the wind, so there are casualties if the wind is behind them and they come to a fence. The front ones halt but those behind push on, scrambling on top of the first lot, "as the cavalry did in the Battle of Waterloo, so we call a fence where that has happened a Waterloo point, and of course a shepherd rushes to hack it down if he sees a flock heading towards it." Yes, he said the unpredictability of Falkland weather made it impossible to avoid some losses through cramps after shearing, but if shearing was not started by a certain time the seasonal routine fell behind. On the other hand, a manager may start shearing because the weather is mild, then the temperature drops and there can even be snow.

The *Darwin* had moved further out, because of the tide, I suppose, and we passengers had to get into a motor launch. The jetty was still crowded with stuff that had been brought from Stanley. Aluminium roofing for a pre-fabricated house lay in a pile of ridged sheets, and when the wind blew of couple of these into the sea, the launch had to retrieve them with a boat hook —a tricky business but very necessary. Two flat-bottomed cargo boats, called scows, were full and formed a kind of raft because they were lashed together. They were then attached by rope to the launch. We set off with them in tow to reach the ship.

At dinner, conversation between Mr. Jones the Mate, Paul Charman and myself was concerned with the Argentine republic and her claims concerning the Falklands. There was news that at the United Nations Lord Caradon had promised Argentina that talks on improved communications between that country and the Falklands should be held. At least this was the rumour, but Sir Cosmo Haskard, Governor of the Falklands, was due to make a broadcast that evening. Mr. Jones knew Argentina as well as Uruguay, although he had not been to the part that particularly interests me, the hundred-year-old Welsh colony in Chubut, Patagonia. The colony did still retain its Welsh customs and ways, and the people spoke Welsh, though they had to learn Spanish as well. He knew a Welsh woman who taught in a school there, and he lent me some

travel brochures about Chubut, which I perused until everyone
—that is the two passengers, some of the *Darwin's* officers, crew,
and stewards, all came into the lounge to listen to the Governor
on the radio.

After some introductory remarks, he read out the text of Lord
Caradon's letter to U. Thant, Secretary General of the United
Nations, and this stated what we knew already, namely, that
early next year there would be "Special talks with a view to
reaching agreement on practical measures for the implementa-
tion and promotion of free communications and movement in
both directions between the mainland and the Islands". Sir
Cosmo again emphasized that while a relaxation on present
restriction of communication would be excellent, the talks would
be held "without prejudice to the position of either country on
the question of sovereignty. This means that the British Government's position . . . remains unchanged, namely that there can
be no transfer of sovereignty over the Falkland Islands against
the wishes of the people of these Islands".

Nobody had much to say after the broadcast. Falkland
Islanders have heard this promise again and again, but they
still fear consent to change of sovereignty may be forced upon
them eventually, though most of them do not think it will
happen for a few years. Yet no-one denies that sailings to
Gallegos, instead of the 1,000 miles to Montevideo, would make
their islands less isolated.

I woke next morning to find the *Darwin* was in Fox Bay,
midway between the two settlements, one lying on the east side
of the harbour and the other on the west. Both farms belong to
the F.I.C. Fox Bay is on the West Falkland, and its name refers
to the wild fox *(Canis antarcticus)*, the only quadruped found
on the islands when they were first discovered, but which
became extinct before the end of the nineteenth century. Darwin
called it a wolflike fox and in 1833 said its numbers were declining. "They are already banished from that half of the island
which lies eastward of the neck of land between St. Salvador
Bay and Berkeley Sound. Within a very few years after these
islands shall have become regularly settled, in all probability
the fox will be classed with the dodo, as an animal which has
perished from the face of the earth." Darwin did not visit the
West Falkland, but one assumes the fox or 'warrah' was found

in large numbers once around Fox Bay. In 1837, Admiral Grey notes in his diary that he saw one at Port Edgar, a harbour a dozen miles south.

Mr. Jones told me at breakfast that Paul Charman had gone ashore with Mr. Vinson and Mr. Gilruth to Fox Bay East in a launch that left at six o'clock, but there would be one at nine o'clock for Fox Bay West. I should not have long there because Captain Miller wanted to sail before midday. I was sorry I had missed the chance of Fox Bay East because Annie Bonner was now housekeeper to the manager and I would have liked to see her again. Fox Bay West was a pretty settlement, hilly, more picturesque than the ones I had seen yesterday, and with hedges of gorse in bloom and the grass thick with daisies. I wandered around with my camera and two small children begged me to take a photograph of them, which I did after asking their names. They were Jeanie and Frankie. An adorable sheepdog puppy kept following me and once he sat and posed so perfectly that I had to take a picture of him. I ended my visit with a call on the manager's wife, Mrs. Robertson, who welcomed me warmly.

The *Darwin* was next making for Port Stephens because she had a prefabricated house to deliver. I spent a pleasant afternoon, wrapped up in padded jacket, on deck, watching the beautiful scenery as we passed the entrance to Port Edgar, the Arch Islands, and Cape Meredith, the most south-westerly point of the Falklands. From the sea I saw the archway—which gives the Arch Islands its name—perfectly, far better than from the plane. For company I had flying overhead king shags and giant petrels, known as 'stinkers' owing to their musty smell. After tea we turned to the right and sailed along an inlet—quite 10 miles in length—at the head of which lay Port Stephens. This farm was first owned by J. M. Dean and passed to the F.I.C. when Dean sold out to the Company in 1889. It was then, and still is, the most important sheep station on West Falkland. Captain Miller hoped to get the *Darwin* right up to the jetty, as being alongside meant loading could take place directly to the ship, without using scows and launch, but all depended on the depth of water. However, he managed it. I found the jetty was lined with empty drums and other freight so, having climbed from the ship down a ladder (not a rope one!) I had to make my way over these objects. Here again I was entertained by the manager's wife, Mrs. Gosse. Loading and unloading were still in operation when I returned, and I waited for a lull before the ladder was put for my convenience. When I got over the ship's side, it was necessary to climb over the empty drums that were now on board, and one of the crew remarked, "You'll be quite a sailor soon."

Early next day we were due at Trieste, an uninhabited island, off the East Falkland coast and lying midway between North Arm and Goose Green. Here we were to collect sheep that had been put on the island to fatten themselves up on tussac grass before being slaughtered for mutton at Stanley. Shepherds from Goose Green were coming in a schooner, the *Penelope*, to round them up, so the gathering would not begin until they arrived.

There was no sign of *Penelope* when *Darwin* anchored off Trieste, a lovely picture of long yellow beach, black rocks with the background of the amazing green tussac. The companion-way was down and Paul told me the launch was about to start as some of the crew meant to shoot kelp geese while waiting. Paul was a keen botanist and he heard there was a type of orchid on the other side of the island. So we both got into the launch and it skimmed across the stretch of calm, grey-blue, kelp-filled water. There was no proper landing place. The launch got as near the beach as possible and then one was expected to wade, but as I had not got Wellington boots, one of the crew hoisted me on his back. Meanwhile some of the men with rifles had already made their way across the sand and were climbing among the tussac when they disturbed a sea lion having a nap by a root of the grass. He emerged and floundered over sand and rocks until he plunged into the sea.

Paul said that sea lions were not aggressive, but I ought always to take care that I did not stand between the creature and the sea as it might panic and rush for the water. Sea lions move with great swiftness and a human could be crushed as though by a steam roller. According to Admiral Grey, "If they are hard pressed they will turn about and raise their body up with their fore-fins and face you standing with their mouth wide open upon their guard." We walked past a group of wives with their lord lying stretched on the sand, drowsily enjoying the sunshine. The bull uttered a few lazy snorts and the cows gazed at us with luscious dark brown eyes, so melting and woe-begone. Their coats were a much lighter brown than I expected and the single pup even lighter. He was the only one I saw, an out-of-season baby, and probably at the teenage stage. As soon as we approached he made off for the sea, but the adults did not stir.

Further along we found the nest of an oyster-catcher with two pale blueish-white eggs mottled with dark brown. The nest was on the ground and had stones scooped round it. Then we saw a quark, who did not move and gave me an opportunity of seeing his lovely colouring and characteristic flowing pennant feather streaming from the back of his head. Gulls, kelp geese and other birds were there in profusion.

I knew Paul was anxious to add to his flower collection by finding the orchid and as I did not fancy a long walk across the tussac, I insisted on him leaving me. Then I scrambled back over rocks and sat down to watch a group of sea lions. A couple of cows were flicking themselves with the 'fingers' of their webbed flippers—exactly like those of a frogman—and one sweet creature was daintily scratching her forehead. Two, darker brown in colour, were reared up on their bellies, so that chests, necks, and heads were clear of the ground, and with their mouths wide open they were scolding each other. Every now and then, one would fall prone but raise her tail in rage. The bull ignored them. He was much too occupied in receiving the amorous attentions of another wife who was nuzzling him and rubbing her body against his. After a time he started to stroke her and soon they were caressing each other.

The sky became overcast so I returned to the *Darwin* as soon as the launch came back. The *Penelope* had still not arrived, and did not do so until after lunch. During the meal Mr. Jones told me that if the gathering and shipping of the Trieste sheep were not finished before dark, we might have to spend the night anchored off Motley Island where more sheep were to be collected, and then we should not reach Stanley until Monday afternoon. There were about 1,000 sheep on Trieste, and each scow could only carry fifty at a time, so loading would take a few hours.

When this began I had a grandstand view of the front cargo deck from the windows of the lounge. I could even see the scows approaching the *Darwin* with their fifty sheep apiece. In each scow was a crate containing ten sheep, the rest being loose, and the crate was hoisted into the air. The sheep looked very miserable but unpleasantly passive and resigned to their fate. I never heard a single "baa". As a crate was swung down into the open hold, a seaman let the sheep out one by one because Mr. Jones had to keep an accurate account of the number for the F.I.C. to assess the freight charges, that I think were 5s. per sheep. The empty crate was swung back into the scow and more sheep packed into it—not always an easy job, for obstinate ones would even get underneath. Meanwhile, down the hold, after every scowload, the seaman was busy marshalling sheep into rows. It was pathetic the way they stood, deprived of their usual occupation of nibbling grass and therefore looking so dejected. When the hold was full, the operation moved to the other end of the ship, but it was still very slow. The crate had to come over and back either five or six times—for not always could ten fat sheep be packed into it. After both scows were unloaded, the launch took them back to Trieste for the next consignment—about ten in all. I think the *Darwin* finally got away from the island at half-past five, and as the men had agreed to work until midnight, she went to Motley, preceded by the *Penelope*, and the loading of the sheep there went on in spite of darkness. There were only 350 to be collected from the second island.

Two sheep died and it was a gruesome sight to watch them being skinned on deck and the carcases tossed overboard. Before I disembarked at Stanley next morning, I waited for the sheep to be let out. They were out of the hold and assembled on deck, and as the companionway was lowered, they walked down it and along the jetty, but the gates at the end were closed, the only exit being through a shed and from there, I conclude, to the slaughter house. I was already beginning to dislike mutton and I felt I should be even less ready to eat any after seeing the happenings of yesterday. But oh, the mess and stink! I had to pick my way carefully down a companionway slippery with sheep dung. Seamen were already at work hosing the holds.

The most popular and the best-known nature reserve in the Falklands is Kidney Island that lies 8 miles by sea from Stanley. It is a small island of about 73 acres and on it have been recorded as breeding no fewer than twenty-five different species of birds, including three kinds of penguins—the jackass, the rockhopper and the macaroni. Parties of schoolchildren from the Stanley schools are taken there each summer, and it is also a popular picnic place with adults who are mildly interested in the birds, while a serious ornithologist like Ian Strange goes there repeatedly to observe and to ring. Ian promised to take me to Kidney Island, but he found it difficult to fix a date, partly because he had to hire a boat—his own being at West Point Island—and partly because of weather difficulties. The day must be calm or one cannot land. In the end. I had the opportunity to join at the last minute a party of B.A.S. men who were staying in Stanley prior to going 'on the ice'—the phrase for going to do scientific work in Antarctica or one of the Antarctic island bases. There were six men, Roz Barnes and myself, and between us we hired a government launch, the *Alert*, for £11, not being certain until the morning of sailing whether or not the weather would be fit for Kidney Island. So often it is not.

The approach to the island was very similar to Trieste. The sandy beach was more white than yellow, but there were the same black rocks and immediately above the shore was the same pale-green growth of tussac. From a distance tussac reminds one of stunted, thickly-bunched palms, in the way the tufts of long grass shoots droop down from thick pedestals of roots. After transferring from launch to dinghy, then from dinghy wading ashore—and this time I was wearing Wellington boots —we climbed up to the tussac and found a clear path between plants. This led to a hut where Ian Strange often stays for several days when studying birds there. It was rather dreary, just equipped with table, four straw-covered bunks, and a Stanley No. 8 range, but the last-named had a notice that it was out of order and must not be lit on any account. However we were able to dump our lunch bags there before making our way to the other side of the island where we were told we should see rockhopper penguins and king shags nesting. There had been some dozen jackass penguins on the beach, inspecting us as we arrived.

Although the majority of people only see penguins in zoos, I have never met anyone who failed to be fascinated by them. To see them in their natural surroundings and completely free is a thousand times more exciting, and I shall always be thankful for the Falkland Islands giving me this opportunity—as well as many other unique experiences.

Rockhopper penguins are about half the size of gentoos and they have a streak of yellow feathers slanting upwards above each eye until it ends in a tuft above the ear. Both they and the jackass are very curious. A number of 'rockies' were sunning themselves on a rock but deliberately climbed nearer and nearer, obviously to observe me more closely. I saw how appropriate was their name for they did hop from rock to rock, and though there could not have been any grip in their webbed feet, yet they seemed to maintain a steady position. Five took a few clumsy steps even nearer. Then two turned round as if studying the view out to sea, while the other three stared. I felt I was in the presence of Dr. Fu Manchu and a couple of his attendants, for the slanting yellow above-the-eye feathers give the rock-hopper an oriental look.

Both 'rockies' and jackasses were nesting amid the tussac so one had to walk carefully to avoid getting anywhere near chicks, for the parents would give vicious jabs at one's ankles to ward off the danger. I saw several rockhopper babies, but the jackass ones were hidden underground, this species having the unusual penguin habit of nesting in burrows. Apart from the birds, it is exhausting to push one's way through masses and masses of tussac. The paths are so narrow, often blocked by growth, and the pedestals so thick and the hanging blades of grass so plenteous—and moreover the height prevents one seeing over the top—I began to feel as though I were lost in an intricate maze. I was very glad to get out. I am sure one could easily get tussac-panic.

It was cool and shady there, but I emerged into hot sunshine and as I looked at the vivid bright blue sea and felt the sun's warmth, it seemed unbelievable that I was only a few hundred miles off Cape Horn. After eating my lunch I lay on the beach for most of the afternoon, watching the jackass penguins. Parental duties were keeping them busy. Either the mother or the father would remain guarding the chicks in the burrow, while the other toiled through the tussac and climbed down the sandy slope to the beach, across the beach and into the sea, where he or she caught and ate fish, returning full of food that would be regurgitated into the open beaks of hungry offspring; but there was always time to chat to fellow penguins on the way, or so it seemed. I watched penguins advancing towards the sea and penguins returning from the sea, and they would meet, bow to one another and make the peculiar braying noise of the jackass penguin. Quaint little old men, waiters in black dress suits with white shirt fronts—such descriptions may be hackneyed but they come back into one's mind when watching the birds. Sometimes their behaviour is quite unexplicable. I saw two meet, and the one who had just come from the sea, turned round and rushed back into the water. Of course, sea is the penguin's true element and it is a joy to watch his swift, graceful swimming.

I saw other birds besides penguins. There were the rapacious turkey buzzards, black, vulture-like creatures, and one that flew overhead had a lamb dangling from his talons. The jackasses were scared of the turkey buzzards and would dash into the sea until they had passed. A tussac bird, which belongs to the family of ovenbirds and is like a small dark brown thrush, came and pecked at some crusts I threw down. There were plenty of logger ducks and kelp geese about. One of the B.A.S. men came to say he had found a nest with a kelp goose sitting on eggs.

There were sea lions swimming around, and one, obviously a bull because of his size, was tearing across the bay by himself, his huge body moving up and down in the water making dark humps that looked like pictures of the supposed Loch Ness monster. As we were being rowed to the *Alert* we saw that he was following our small boat and he came quite close. Twice he raised his head clear of the water, showing face and whiskers, and he roared at us. This was unusual and one of the men thought he had been wounded in a fight with a rival bull, and the boatman—a Kelper—remarked, "Something has made him mad. He is in a real temper." Anyway, he decided we were not worth attacking and slackened his pace. Before we got aboard the *Alert* he had disappeared under the water.

Then came the sail back to Stanley, which took an hour and a quarter and was enlivened by the sight of a few dolphins gambolling past. Instinctively one thinks of a dolphin as playful, as one thinks of a penguin as amusing. A cow sea-lion, I should say, was appealing, but after the angry bull at Kidney Island, I could only apply the adjectives 'wrathful' and 'irascible' to the males.

8

Midsummer

I RETURNED from this short coastal trip on 23rd November, and in my diary for the following day I noted the sunny mild weather that Stanley people regarded as a heat wave. Although in the streets women were wearing cotton frocks, often without cardigans, and a few small children were even in sunsuits, I clung to woollen blouse, slacks, and quilted jacket, and was glad of them. Nor could I truthfully agree when someone said, "Gee, but it is hot!" You might have thought the Falklands lay in the tropics by the way every window of every house was wide open, but for once the god of winds, Aeolus, was giving Stanley a miss, and I could go out minus headscarf without having hair blown over my face or streaming behind. The gardens were very gay now, so colourful with lupins, snapdragons, red and yellow daisies, and even pansies, but the daffodils were over and the gorse was less bright than when I first arrived. Many houses have glass porches, and in these grew geraniums and roses in profusion.

December is the equivalent of June in the northern hemisphere, 24th December being Midsummer Day, and such is the changeableness of the Falklands climate that in a diary entry for 10th December I wrote "very cold wind", while on the evening of 21st December, "the ground is white with sleet." According to official reports, this December in Stanley was the sunniest for ten years with highest temperatures since 1963. "The highest recorded temperature during the month was 20·4° C. (68·8° F.) on the 27th, and the lowest was 1·0° C. (33·8° F.) on the nights of the 19th and 22nd. . . . There were six nights on which ground frost was recorded at the site of the Stanley Meteorological Station."

8th December, anniversary of the Battle of the Falkland Islands, is a bank holiday. The Governor first goes to a commemorative service at the Cathedral, then proceeds to the Town Hall, where, standing outside, he takes the salute from a marching parade of Hovercraft, Royal Marines, Local Defence Force and Girls Brigade. For this occasion he wears uniform and hat with white plumes. I heard that the plumes were fastened into place by a clip and once a governor's valet did not secure the clip properly so the plumes fell off at a crucial moment. I expected the Governor to be by the Battle Memorial for the march past, but this can be such an unpleasantly windy spot that the town hall is preferred.

The memorial is half a mile further along Ross Road and near the water's edge. It consists of a granite pedestal, 35 feet high. On top of this is a graceful bronze model of a sixteenth-century ship, "the type of ship contemporary with discovery of the Falkland Islands and is intended to symbolize the beginning of the British Navy". It was unveiled in February 1927, after being erected by public subscription, and the inscription reads, "In commemoration of the Battle of the Falkland Islands, fought on the 8th day of December 1914, in which the British Squadron *Invincible, Inflexible, Carnarvon, Kent, Cornwall, Glasgow, Bristol, Canopus,* and *Macedonia,* under the command of Vice-Admiral Sir F. C. Doveton Sturdee, K.C.B., C.V.O., C.M.G., destroyed the German Squadron under Vice-Admiral Graf von Spee. . . ." Above the inscription is a figure of Victory and she is facing the direction where the battle was fought. Besides saving the colony from capture by the Germans, this engagement gave Britain mastery of the South Atlantic, an important factor in her favour for the rest of the war.

The Battle Memorial is Stanley's only piece of sculpture. The Falkland Islands Company put up a Whalebone Arch in 1951 to commemorate the Company's centenary. This consists of the jawbones of two whales, and is enclosed by a small green with seats round the base of the arch. Inconspicuous—in fact I failed to discover it—is a brass plate along the wall beside the public jetty. This bears the inscription "ALFRED 24th February 1871", and records the visit of Queen Victoria's second son, Alfred Duke of Edinburgh, who called when on board H.M.S. *Galatea.* The only other member of the Royal Family ever to visit the

Falklands is our present Duke of Edinburgh. It was intended that the naval vessel on which George V and his brother, the Duke of Clarence, were serving as midshipmen should call, but the ship had an urgent message to proceed somewhere else so was forced to sail past. No British monarch has ever set foot on this Crown Colony of the Falkland Islands.

The Cathedral has two memorials to the work of Bishop Stirling. These are the chancel screen and the east window. In the stained-glass pictures of the latter, below a figure of St. Nicholas, is the mission schooner, *Allen Gardiner*. There were three successive ships of this name, and the first brought Stirling and other missionaries from England to Keppel Island off West Falkland. At the bottom of the window is the inscription, "To the Glory of God and in Memory of Waite Hockin Stirling, First Bishop of the Falkland Islands."

During December I tried to see various officials to find out all I could about government of the islands, and I did my best to supplement this information by examining records, but this was exceptionally difficult. The Colonial Secretary permitted me to inspect the Secretariat archives but he warned me that a large number had perished in the town hall fire, while much of the remainder needed sorting and classifying. I spent several mornings in this room and enjoyed myself, though to very little purpose.

Another hindrance to research was the absence of a local newspaper. The excellent *Falkland Islands Journal* is an annual concerned with history. There was a *Falkland Islands Magazine* issued from the Cathedral from 1889 to 1927, but this was more in the nature of a church magazine. Neither did I find three other short-lived periodicals very helpful, the last one ceasing in 1949, when there was nothing until the *Falkland Islands Monthly Review* started on 5th December 1958. It still appears and is a twenty-page publication that allots a great deal of space to sport fixtures and teams, dances, weddings, births, deaths, lists of new goods in the shops, and shipping information. I managed to borrow the only complete file in existence from the first editor, Mr. Hirtle, and in this—especially in the earlier numbers—I did find articles and information that were very useful. From this source I learnt about the ill-fated mink farm, comments on a report on road-making possibilities, and

H

eye-witness accounts of Lord Chalfont's visit, and the attempted Condor 'liberations'.

In an issue for 7th October 1968, I came across a reference to a novel dealing with the Falklands, the first time I knew one had ever been written. It was by a woman called Theo Gift, though there was no indication if this was her real or an assumed name, "About 1896 she wrote a book *An Island Princess*, a story about a Falkland Islands girl." This intrigued me. I thought that here I might get a picture of what life on the islands was like at the end of the nineteenth century, and my search for a copy developed into a sort of detective hunt, for nobody except Miss Biggs, the librarian, had ever seen a copy and she had read the novel long ago and could not remember much about it. She borrowed it from the late Dr. Forrest McWhan, a local historian with a fine collection of books, but though Miss Biggs asked his widow, Mrs. McWhan knew nothing of the novel and was quite unable to find it. I tried Government House, then asked several likely people. The wife of one retired farm manager thought it might be a book in which Mrs. Orissa Pole-Evans of Port Howard was mentioned. That was the only clue I got and when I saw the lady she said she featured in a non-fiction work, *Sailor at Sea*, reminiscences of a naval man who was stationed on the Falklands for a short time in World War I. So this clue petered out.

I spent a few days in London on my return from the Falklands and as I had a ticket for the British Museum Reading Room, I was at last able to trace the book there, for under the Copyright Acts a copy had been deposited by the publishers. The catalogue showed that Theo Gift was a pseudonym, the author's real name being Dora Havers, and she married a man called Boulger. Between 1875 and 1893 she wrote twenty novels and edited some collections of children's tales. *An Island Princess* appeared in 1893, not 1896.

Plot and characters were feeble. The heroine was a girl of 18 who became secretly engaged to a naval officer and drowned herself when she learnt he had married someone else in England. But as a picture of life on the Falklands eighty years ago, I was surprised to find so much remained unchanged. While there were no B.A.S. nor E.S.R.O. personnel, yet when a naval ship came into Stanley harbour there was the same excitement as during my visit in 1969 over the arrival of H.M.S. *Endurance*. Of course there were no Land-Rovers, only horse transport in Stanley (called Palmerston, while the Falklands were Las Malvinas). Jean Coniston, the heroine, rides everywhere on her mare, Brown Jenny, and when she and the flag-lieutenant hero first meet, she sees him thrown off his horse into a bog, promptly races after the straying horse, and from Brown Jenny's back lassoes it. Later hero rescues heroine from an enraged bull.

The authoress is very depressing about the climate and the remoteness. "Think of an English colony one thousand miles from the nearest point of civilization on the nearest continent . . . swept over and ravaged by blistering winds from every quarter of the compass . . . an island where there are no theatres, no music-halls, no concerts. . . ." She mentions penguins, sea-lions, wrecks, peat bogs, diddle dee, absence of trees, and graphically describes the seaweed around the coast: ". . . strong and brown, and tall and fleshy, whose myriad strands, wreathed and twisted with one another, like the arms of some vegetable octopus, have power to drag down and strangle the strongest swimmer who ever managed to get entangled in their treacherous meshes."

At that period there was a mission for training christian converts from Tierra del Fuegia in the Falklands, on Keppel Island. Theo Gift writes in unflattering terms about these Patagonians, ". . . the squat forms and squalid malignant features of the Indian catechumens labouring sullenly at their work of peat-cutting and potato-hoeing."

I was glad I did eventually manage to trace a copy of this book, although I had to wait until I got back to England. As far as I have been able to discover, it is the only novel set in the Falkland Islands, and after a lapse of nearly eighty years it has a certain historical value. I think it a pity that no copies have been preserved on the islands themselves.

In another back number of the *Monthly Review* (4th May 1964) I found a reference to the hydatid cyst. This is a sac of watery fluid containing minute larvae of a tapeworm. It can only develop through a dog, so, though the growth occurs in sheep and cattle, and it is said cannot be transmitted by those animals to man, yet it can pass from them to dog and from dog to man. The cyst was was first officially reported in 1953 when a veterinary surgeon examined sheep carcases sent to a freezing plant which was then in operation at Ajax Bay, East Falkland. He found 2½ per cent had cysts. Eleven years later, another vet reported an alarming increase, so much so that the Sheepowners' Association ruled that all dogs on farms should be inspected four times a year. "An Inspector has been appointed for each Camp settlement," was the statement in the *Monthly Review* for August 1965, "and drugs and instructions will be forwarded when the number of dogs is known."

Although this was done, control was not nearly strict enough. I was told that many of the older shepherds strongly objected to dosing their dogs and threw away the pills they were supposed to administer. Moreover, enforcement of any regulation is extremely difficult in the isolation of the Camp. It was observed, more or less efficiently, on some farms, but not on others. In 1969, the team of agricultural advisers came from Britain and they speedily discovered the presence of the cyst in a sheep's carcase, drew attention to it, and Stanley became alarmed.

The infection spreads mainly through offal, since the cyst attaches itself to organs like the liver, and in a talk over the local radio, the Box, Mr. McCrea, the veterinary surgeon of the team, emphasized that all offal should be burnt, or safely buried, so that the sheepdogs on a farm could not get at it. Too often in the past sheep would be slaughtered and the offal flung down with the result that they were eaten by the dogs. Mr. McCrea also said there must be systematic dosing against worms. He explained the nature of hydatid disease, how the infection spread, and how Iceland, once very badly affected, had entirely rid itself of the cyst. New Zealand was working towards the same end, and it could be done on the Falklands with regular dosing and proper offal disposal, but it would take several years. He thought the number of farm dogs too high. Apparently it is one to every two humans, but on talking to a former manager I was told that reduction was not practicable since, owing to the rough terrain a dog easily gets sore feet, with the result that every Camp shepherd does need four dogs.

A film from New Zealand, entitled *Dogs Can Be Dangerous*, was shown in Stanley, prior to circulation round the Camp, and I went to see it. I also accepted Mr. McCrea's invitation to members of the public to come to the Hospital laboratory and see specimens he had on view. There was a sheep's liver with cyst growing on it, as well as explanatory diagrams and statistics, while one could ask questions. The telephone kept ringing. One Stanley woman was asking if she could give her pet cat liver because the animal refused to eat anything else. I believe shops were thronged with people buying proprietary brands of pet food in tins—sent from England, and not very popular until now.

Stanley was alarmed, but reaction on the Camp was rather different. Farm managers were ready to co-operate, but there was opposition, or at the best indifference, from many older shepherds. One of the British women was telling me about a visit she had just paid to one of the settlements by ship and how, on going ashore, sheepdogs ran clustering round her and jumping up in their usual friendly fashion.

"I thought, I mustn't touch them because if they lick me they can pass on this worm from the hydatid cyst, so I was trying to get away and of course putting my hands in my pockets because stupidly I had not put on gloves, when an old man called out, 'Don't be frightened! They won't bite you.' I told him I wasn't frightened but I didn't want to catch the disease the Grassmen said dogs caught from sheep and could pass to human beings. 'Oh that! Lot of fuss about nothing! We've known about it for years and the mutton is all the better for these 'ere cysts.' I pointed out that the Grassmen were experts sent specially from the U.K. but I couldn't convince him. He said, 'They don't know what they're talking about. Then cysts make the mutton all the better. We've always eaten 'em with the liver. Leastways I have and I'm all right.' So after that I gave up arguing and went back to the ship."

A programme of Camp education concerning the hydatid disease was being planned, and it included showing of the New Zealand film where settlements had facilities for doing so. Before I left in January 1970, a committee of sixteen was formed to take strong action regarding inspection, insistence on regular dosing of dogs with supervision when possible, and compelling every farm to dispose safely of offal so that dogs could not eat it. Falkland sheep farmers were troubled with scab disease in sheep from 1843 until the end of the century when, with strict measures, the disease was wiped out. The same thing can be done with the hydatid cyst.

This was not the first Christmas I had spent in the southern hemisphere, and, as previously, I found it difficult to get excited over a festival that, to me, came in the wrong season of the year, at midsummer instead of in the depth of winter. Of course it was not like spending Christmas in the tropics. Temperatures on the Falklands were not sufficiently high to give one a distaste for roast turkey, plum pudding and mince pies. I say roast turkey, for British residents keep to the traditional dish and as there are no turkeys reared on the islands they are brought frozen from Montevideo; but the Kelper celebrates the Christmas feast with roast lamb.

There was none of the weeks-ahead shopping for presents as at home, and decorations in the shops were put up just a few days before. When the *Darwin* reached Stanley on 17th December, she brought among her passengers several pupils from the British School in Montevideo. These boys and girls can only come home for the long summer holiday that lasts from mid-December until February. Local schools broke up on 19th December, and for the forty children boarders at Darwin came the business of their transport to different parts of the Camp. Accommodation on a Beaver floatplane is limited to six, so 'breaking-up' meant several extra flights, and the situation was worsened by a high wind forcing down a Beaver at San Salvador and keeping it there for twenty-four hours.

Arrivals on the *Darwin* in December included the Archdeacon, the Venerable J. Gould, and his wife. Like the Bishop, the Archdeacon lives in the centre of the diocese, in Buenos Aires, and he was making this visit to the Falklands to conduct the special commemorative services for the anniversary of the first bishop's consecration. I met the Goulds at the Deanery, and later saw a good deal of them on a Camp trip we both took. I enjoyed listening to Asta Gould describing life in Argentina, and I began to regret I could not return to England via Latin America, but it was impossible to think of changing my A.E.S. reservation at this late date. In any case, I could not have done it, for one could only get to South America by the *Darwin* and she was fully booked from January until the autumn.

There were a few more stamp-sticking sessions and on the last afternoon Jill Millam, Asta Gould and myself were the only ones left. It was half-past six as we finished, and at the same time Peter Millam and the Archdeacon returned from a meeting and insisted on taking us to the newly-opened Upland Goose Hotel for a drink. My childish pleasure at this 'treat' shows how barren of gaiety and entertainment I had begun to find Stanley. There is still a convention that no woman should go to a public house, of which Stanley has three, and until today there had been no hotel with a private bar. 'The Ship' closed before my arrival. Now it was reopened and metamorphosed into the 'Upland Goose', a complete transformation, I had heard. One evening I met the new owners, the Kings, on their return from England, and learnt something of their plans for structural alterations, introduction of a central-heating system, and the new furniture and kitchen equipment being sent out. It was indeed a joy to be taken into the new, attractive, modern without being meretricious, private bar, and as I sipped my drink I felt transported back into a familiar, colourful, urban world.

I realized then that I was getting very tired of the dull monotony of Stanley, that I really was homesick and thankful I was leaving in January, not waiting until April as at first I intended. I did regret, and still do, that I was unable to accept various Camp invitations I received, and this regret was intensified by the two *Darwin* trips I took immediately after Christmas. The Camp was lively and friendly. There was none of the stiff aloofness one often encountered in Stanley. The 'capital' is all right for a few weeks, but it has not enough to offer the visitor for a longer spell. Certainly a good modern hotel, that at last it has, will be an asset. Although I did not stay at the 'Upland Goose', I saw the newly furnished rooms and I sampled Mrs. King's delicious cooking when Roz Barnes and I entertained to dinner Jill, Asta and Margaret Owens.

Overseas Christmas mail arrived by *Darwin* on 17th December. On such occasions one could wait for delivery by postman, or rather postwoman, but most people went personally to the post office as soon as the Box put out an announcement that mail was ready for collection. The post office staff were quite quick in unpacking the bags and sorting letters, and the announcement would come in a couple of hours after a ship's arrival. Newspapers that one had ordered previously could be collected from Joan Bound's shop, and by now I was so desperate for news— British news—that I did not mind them being weeks behind. One cannot get the B.B.C. Home Service on radio, only the B.B.C. Overseas, which gives international news, and I was longing to hear about happenings in Britain, even the kind of weather.

Absence of newspapers, or the long delay, does not worry the Kelper. What you never have, you never miss. One man told me that when he visited England and his brother first handed him a morning newspaper at breakfast, he simply could not believe he was reading about events that only occurred the day before. The same Kelper also confessed how nervous of trains he felt, his knowledge of them being confined to what he learnt at school at Stanley. "And you always hear of train crashes so imagine these are constantly happening, and when you actually travel in one, conditioned thus from childhood, you expect it to crash."

I was very grateful to Lady Haskard, the Governor's wife, for inviting me to "come and dine with us on Christmas night, 25th December itself," and she added that 8 p.m. would be the time for guests to arrive "and it usually tends to be a fairly late evening". Then I was asked to midday dinner by Margaret and Elwyn Owen, this being particularly welcome, for children are an essential part of Christmas and I was very fond of Rachel and Daniel Owen, aged 2 and one years. Margaret served an excellent meal. Afterwards we sat in the lounge over coffee and liquors while Elwyn played operatic and ballet music on his record player. Listening to *Tannhauser*, *Faust* and *The Sleeping Beauty*, I decided that one of the first things I would do when I got back to London would be to go to Covent Garden for a performance of either an opera or a ballet.

Government House is a patchy affair, with various additions grafted on the original villa that, as far as I could gather, was built in 1864, but it is not the gracious residence that one expects to be provided for the Queen's representative. However, it is comfortably furnished, has central heating, and along one side is a long glass conservatory which gives a beautiful view of the gardens, of the harbour, and of the hills behind. At one cocktail party I attended it was a lovely evening, and as I looked through a window at the clear waters, greenish-blue under a bright blue sky, I could fancy I was on the island of Torcello gazing out on the Venetian lagoon.

Fourteen guests had been invited to the Christmas night party, and they included five staying in the house—the Goulds, who had now left the Deanery; Sir Gerald Lathbury, ex-Governor of Gibraltar; and a Dr. Malone and his wife just returned from leave. At dinner I was put next to the Archdeacon, while on my right was Mr. Johnston, head of E.S.R.O. in Stanley, and through becoming acquainted with him that evening I later had the privilege of being shown over the space research station. We had a wonderful Christmas dinner, a positive banquet. Lady Haskard was a delightfully jolly hostess and Sir Cosmo a most attentive host. As is usual at a Government House dinner, the Royal Toast was given and drunk with much enthusiasm, but otherwise there was little formality or protocol that night.

We spent the remainder of the evening playing games. First we had decorous word ones in the drawing-room, more energetic ones in the billiard-room, and then we returned to the drawing-room for balancing feats and more drinks. To end the evening we played "Nuts in May" and had a hilarious tug-of-war—childish pastimes, but exactly right for Christmas night.

The chief lady guest, the one who sits on the Governor's right at dinner, has the duty of deciding when to leave—always previously arranged with the Governor's wife. On this occasion the chief lady guest was Mrs. Johnston, wife of the E.S.R.O. chief, and she broke up the party at 2.30 a.m. We said our good-byes as we followed her out, and here I must mention the thoughtfulness of Sir Cosmo in looking after his guests' comfort. When I went to Government House on the island of St. Helena, one had a rough idea of the time of departure and could arrange for a taxi to be waiting, but in Stanley there were no taxis. Sir Cosmo knew I had no car, and he arranged with another guest for me to be driven back to Glasgow Road. I had taken shoes in case I had to tramp the mile-long walk, and though it was a fine night I was very glad to be spared this, especially when wearing a long evening gown.

9

The Machine Ticks Over

WHEN I went to the Falklands I had already visited another British colony, that of St. Helena, so I was acquainted with the system of government through Governor, Executive and Legislative Councils.

The Governor represents the reigning British monarch and his term of office lasts three years, or six if he is willing to stay for a double period. Sir Cosmo Haskard, twenty-first holder of the office, had been appointed in October 1964, and was due to leave the Colony finally in the autumn of 1970. People wondered if he would be replaced now whaling had ceased in the Dependencies, his administrator having been withdrawn from South Georgia and that island left to visiting scientists. The Falkland Islands Dependencies covered South Georgia, South Sandwich Islands, Shag Rocks and Clarke Rocks. The only inhabited island had been South Georgia; that, until evacuation in 1969, had about two dozen permanent residents, the number being swelled during the whaling season, but in 1966 all whaling stations except one were closed, and a caretaker left in charge for another three years. Many Kelpers were now talking about the possibility of the duties of Governor and Colonial Secretary being in future combined in the office of Administrator, while others hoped this would not happen, saying that official entertaining at Government House would then cease and they would miss it.

Photographs of former governors hung in a row along a corridor wall, opposite the library in the town hall, and I often paused to study them from a physiognomic angle. Some looked benign, some irascible; some looked pleasant, some morose; the uniformed ones varied from the Colonel Blimp type to the intelligent military or naval officer. Some mouths were hidden by patriarchal beards or showy moustaches. Some men faced the camera, others gazed indifferently into space. The only one whom I regarded with personal interest was Governor Grey-Wilson (1898–1904) as I had heard about him when I stayed on St. Helena where he was Governor before being appointed to the Falklands. I used to wonder how he bore the change in climate, and what he and his wife thought of their official Stanley residence after St. Helena's beautiful Plantation House. Instead of being the brisk, aristocratic, haughty man I imagined, his appearance in the photograph was that of a kindly Victorian *paterfamilias.*

Administration of the Falkland Islands is under the control of the Legislative Council, of which the Governor is chairman, as well as being supreme authority in matters affecting the Crown—that is directives from the British government. The first Legislative Council for the Falklands was set up on 13th November 1845, but during the years its composition has been altered. It now consists of Governor, Colonial Secretary, Colonial Treasurer, two "independent nominated" members, and four regional members elected by the people. The four public representatives come from West Falkland (one), East Falkland (one) and Stanley (two). The Executive Council, or 'Inner Cabinet' is formed from Governor, Colonial Secretary, Colonial Treasurer, two "independent nominated" members, who seem to be different from those on the larger body, and two of the Legislative Council's public representatives. In 1964 they were Mr. Pitaluga from East Falkland and Major Goss, head of the local Defence Force and aide-de-camp to the Governor, from Stanley. For the Legislative, I noticed a woman, Mrs. N. King, and she was still representing Stanley when I went to a Council meeting in late 1969.

While sessions of the Legislative Council were open to the public, those of the Executive Council were private, though afterwards reported in the *Monthly Review.* This appeared in No. 134, the issue for 2nd February 1970.

Executive Council met on 9th and 10th January for its first meeting of 1970.

Among matters dealt with was the Agreement with Darwin Shipping Company Limited, on the government subsidy to the

Company which carries the mails. The Agreement has been re-negotiated for a term of two years.

Alginate Industries was on the agenda. Negotiations between the Colony Government and the company have reached a stage where it is hoped that it will be possible for a Letter of Intent to be issued to the company in the reasonably near future, which will mean that preparations could begin for the pilot stage of the project.

A new Dogs Order, connected with Hydatid Campaign, was agreed upon and will be issued shortly, simultaneously with a revised list of Inspectors appointed under the Dogs Ordinance. Mr. S. Miller, Chairman of the Campaign Committee, recently broadcast asking for the co-operation of farm Managers, to ensure that replies, to invitations from government sent to individuals to undertake the duties of Inspectors, were sent to the Secretariat as soon as possible. To date, approximately 18 out of 32 persons addressed have replied. It is encouraging that, so far, every reply has been an acceptance.

During my stay on the Falkland Islands, I attended two meetings of the Legislative Council, one on 29th October and the other on 17th December. They were held in the town hall, in a wood-panelled room with a platform at one end, and here, under the royal coat of arms with photographs of the Queen and the Duke of Edinburgh on either side, sat the Governor. The council members were grouped round a table below the platform, while there were ten rows of chairs for the public to occupy, probably accommodation for 150 people. About thirty were present the first time and included officials like the Superintendent of Education. It was a horribly cold day, but the room was quite comfortable with its central heating until the Governor ordered two windows to be opened, and then the warm air was slowly dispersed. Along one side sat two policemen. Below the platform on the Governor's left was the senior chaplain and he opened the proceedings with prayers. Business consisted of proposal and seconding (alternately by Colonial Secretary and Colonial Treasurer) of a number of laws and orders that required formal approval; also an address by the Governor. His Excellency dealt with fluctuation of wool prices; hope of improved productivity following the expected recommendations from the five agricultural advisers (the 'Grassmen'); latest negotiations with Alginate

Industries about establishment of a kelp industry; that six cruise ships were scheduled to call during the summer, he being optimistic "that the Falkland Islands would in time benefit from the world-wide growth of the tourist industry"; the high cost of a possible airfield on the Cape Pembroke peninsula and that, "arising out of the airfield report it was intended that a thorough re-examination of the colony's air and sea transport problems should be carried out to decide what the colony's long-term plans in this respect should be"; the possibility of communications with Argentina being opened and "a gradual removal of artificial barriers"; and finally the state of the colony's finances. "The deficit on the Ordinary Revenue and Expenditure account for the year ended 30th June 1969 was £85,000 and, while this represented a useful improvement on the revised estimate of £103,000, it would be idle to regard it as anything but a serious slice out of our reserves."

The Falkland Islands only receives grants from Britain under the Colonial Development and Welfare scheme which is made for repairs to public buildings, or the building of new ones, like a school. During the years 1965 to 1967, £42,664 in all was received, and this included £18,270 towards purchase of the government cargo vessel the *Forrest*. Otherwise the islands 'run themselves' out of their own revenue. Cost of living is not by any means high and income tax is low in comparison with Britain, a man in receipt of from £4,000 to £6,000 a year paying 4s. 6d. in the pound, and a man with an income exceeding £6,000 paying 5s. 9d. Companies were paying 5s. 9d. per pound (flat rate), but a new rate for them was introduced at the second meeting of the Legislative Council that I attended, when the first reading took place of a Bill to amend income-tax orders. Such services as education, public health, justice, public works (except scavenging and street lighting), water supply, air service, posts and telecommunications, broadcasting, customs and general administration, all come directly under the Government, but Stanley Town Council, the only local government body, is responsible for a few other services.

Having been employed by several local authorities in Britain, I have attended innumerable town council meetings as an official, and there members of the public are also admitted, so I naturally expected to go to a Stanley Town Council meeting without any trouble. A Legislative Council Member told me this was impossible, that the public were never admitted. Foolishly I accepted this statement without question and then tried to find out all I could about the body. It consisted of nine —three members nominated by the Governor and six public elected members from different parts of Stanley. The council each year chose a chairman from among its members. The only official was a town clerk, but not like we have in Britain. This was not a legal man, but just a clerk, and in 1969 was a young girl with shorthand and typing qualifications. I learnt that a Mr. John Lennan, a clerk in the F.I.C. cashier's office, had once been town clerk, and I asked him various questions concerning the Stanley Town Council's activities. He saw no reason why I should not attend a meeting, "only no-one ever does". I wanted to know how the townspeople of Stanley saw their representatives were carrying out their duties, and learnt that there was very little public interest, voting numbers being very poor on the rare occasions there was a contest. Since the council was formed in 1948, there had been no more than three contests, although councillors only served four years, two retiring every two years. Mr. Lennan said meetings were held on the first Monday of every month at 2.15 p.m., and if I really wanted to attend the next (5th January) I had better contact the chairman, a Mr. Phil Summers, who worked in the Secretariat.

The council's income is derived from rates, a government grant of £825, and money made through hire of the town hall. In 1967 the total was £7,651. Rates are 3s. 6d. in the pound, plus a water rate of 1s. which is augmented by sale of water to visiting ships. One of its services is the fire brigade, recently equipped with a new foam tender. In fact it came on the A.E.S. when I travelled to the Falklands, and was soon reported in the *Monthly Review* to have been in action "after a late-night call in the vicinity of the rubbish dump, where a deep-rooted fire seemed likely to creep towards the dairy". I remember one afternoon being disturbed in my reading by an unexpected announcement over the Box. "Good afternoon. This is a practice fire alarm. The practice fire is at Dobbyns Bakery. Thank you." Electric light in Stanley is partly the concern of the town council, but partly that of the Government, the latter owning the diesel power station. The town council is entirely responsible for refuse collection, town hall and library, cemetery, and the upkeep of Arch Green. In 1967, only £464 was spent on the Stanley Library, including librarian's salary. She is part-time. This left very little for book expenditure, certainly not more than £250 per annum, which seemed to me a shockingly small amount in comparison with public libraries in Britain, until I worked it out per head of population, and, as there are only 1,000 people in Stanley, it did come to 5s. per capita, about the same as an English urban district council would spend, only, because no single 1,000 people would have a separate library, the total would be far greater. In considering Falkland Islands financial figures, one has to keep on reminding oneself that the entire population is just a little over 2,000, about the same as the Scilly Isles, and between one tenth and one eleventh that of the Shetland Isles.

After talking to Mr. Lennan, I went to the Secretariat and saw Mr. Summers, chairman of the Stanley Town Council. He appeared to be very astonished that I should want to attend a meeting but gave permission, and I verified the date of 5th January, three weeks hence. When I got to the town hall then, I could find no indication of a meeting in any of the empty rooms, hunted around and at last found someone who went to make enquiries. "Yes, there should be a meeting but nobody seems to be here." Eventually he returned to inform me that it had been postponed a week because the town clerk's grandfather had died, so the chairman and council were attending the funeral, but it would be held on the following Monday. This was three days before I was due to sail, but I managed to go, and I was certainly received with great courtesy, and put at a table where I could sit and make notes.

Unfortunately I could not hear the very low soft voice of the town clerk, and as she read the minutes of the previous meeting from a written minute book without any printed or typed summary being placed before us, I missed the drift of most of that. Among the matters arising was a letter concerning an estimate for repairing part of the cemetery wall. Items discussed that afternoon were: rates on St. Mary's and the Deanery; hiring of town hall and need for a deposit to be paid by hirers beforehand; provision of new lorries for public works; the problem of rats; and the sending of parcels of books to the Camp from the library.

I was not successful in managing to attend one of the law courts, which are, the Supreme Court, the Court of Summary Jurisdiction and the Civil Court, all meeting in Stanley. To quote from the Biennial Report, "The colony retains the part-time services in England of a Legal Adviser. Local ordinances and regulations are in effect. English law applies down to 1900 and subsequently by special application. Some farm managers are Justices of the Peace, as are also certain residents of Stanley, and they have the power to deal with minor offences." In 1967, a Civil Court dealt with forty-eight offences. There were thirty-two for debt, ten for income-tax misdemeanours, one removal of driving disqualification, one maintenance order, one for access to children, and three other cases. The Court of Summary Jurisdiction covered cases of assault, larceny, offences against local ordinances, and breaches of the peace; while the Supreme Court had twenty-one cases—including divorce, bankruptcy, debt, wounding and appeals.

Edward Wilson in his *Diary*, published in 1904, about his Antarctic experiences, refers to a then custom in the Falklands of displaying in the town a black-list of offenders. I do not know when this ceased. The small prison had three male prisoners in 1966, none in 1967, three in 1968. One of these was given a three-year sentence lasting from 1968 to 1970, but in the beginning of 1970 he was sent to Britain, with two policemen in charge, on the same ship as I travelled back, because he was declared to be in need of psychiatric treatment. I believe too that long-term prisoners are sometimes sent to Montevideo; and many years ago, as I heard on St. Helena, they used to go to that island. The police force consists of a superintendent of police, one sergeant, one senior constable, and four others. The superintendent is also the Government fire precautions officer and the immigration and Customs officer.

As regards education, no-one could have been more helpful than the chief officer, Mr. Draycott. He showed me his headquarters, explained the system thoroughly, took me to the Stanley senior school, where the headmaster of this and the junior-infants conducted me round both buildings; and arrangements were made for me to visit the Darwin boarding school,

Fox Bay West settlement

Chartres Estuary, West Falkland

Bales of wool ready for loading. Sometimes the *Darwin* can reach the jetty *(above)*. At other times the wool is loaded into scows *(below)*

only I was unable to do so because of an earlier return to Britain than I first planned.

The chief superintendent of education—to give him his correct title—has spent nearly thirty years on the Falkland Islands. He has a difficult task, especially in the Camp, where, though illiteracy is practically ended, yet scattered communities, uncertainty of transport, shortage of qualified staff, and lack of enthusiasm among many parents over their children's education, all combine to hinder progress. Mr. Draycott praised the understanding and generosity of the Falkland Islands government, but there was a limit to what they could do. The 1968 to 1969 estimates allowed £66,000 for the service, a large sum when one realizes there are only 380 children on the whole of the Falkland Islands, including Stanley. It shows how the youthful population has declined, when in 1886 there were 600 under 15 years of age, although the total figure was 500 less than today. Obviously, the proportion of elderly and middle-aged people is now far greater. Cost of education per child per annum varies from £98 in the Camp to £104 in Stanley and £318 at Darwin boarding school. Allowances to children at school in England and in the British school in Montevideo total £4,000. The Commonwealth Office gives financial assistance towards cost of new school buildings and pays half the fares of teachers coming from Britain to work on contract for four years. There are eight of these at present. The total number of teachers on the islands is thirty-seven, of whom sixteen are certificated, and in addition three Voluntary Service Overseas young men come to give unpaid assistance—chiefly in the Camp. All Camp teachers attend a seminary held at Darwin every September.

The headquarters in Stanley consisted of two rooms in the Secretariat building, and here worked the Superintendent and his clerk. There was no other staff. In the clerk's room was a collection of juvenile books suitable for school libraries and sent by the British Council. Stocks of stationery were also kept here, and they had to be ordered in large supply because of the long time taken on the journey from England. Mr. Draycott's office was equipped with radio, a radio talking machine and tape recorder. He explained how he maintained radio contact with teachers and broadcast educational talks from prepared tapes that he obtained on loan. The 1969 programme showed great variety, from "Great Moments in Science" to "Elementary Book-keeping", from "Journeys Round the World" to "Music and How It Is Made".

Regarding Camp visits, Mr. Draycott said he only went in an emergency, since a visit to an isolated settlement meant he was cut off from contact with schools and teachers, while he might be windbound and unable to return to Stanley for several days. There were full-time schools at Port Howard, Hill Cove, Chartres, Fox Bay East and, of course, Darwin, but otherwise Camp children—until, or if, they went to Darwin—were taught by itinerant teachers, a system he admitted to be unsatisfactory but impossible to alter under the circumstances. I asked him how this home education on the Falklands compared with that in force in the Australian backwoods. That, he said, was carried out by means of radio, the teacher being in communication with every child, so that, although he or she never saw the pupils, lessons were given as to a class and pupils replied to the teacher's questions or asked about their own difficulties. In fact, it is conducted like a class in a school, the only difference being neither teacher nor pupils can see each other.

Then we discussed adult education and the fact that Mr. Draycott found it disheartening to attempt other than 'utilitarian' evening classes for pupils who had recently left school in such subjects as shorthand, typewriting and book-keeping, for which they wanted to take examinations of the Royal Society of Arts. In 1968, there were also three working for City and Guilds, one for Radio Engineers certificate, five for G.E.C. 'O' levels, and two for G.E.C. 'A' levels in two subjects. The only failure was one in the City and Guilds examination. But 'education for leisure' did not catch on in the Falklands, and Mr. Draycott put this down to the hard physical work that men had in the Camp, and to the peat cutting in Stanley. Men were so exhausted in the evenings that the tendency was merely to sit and doze, and the wives followed their example.

I had an interesting morning seeing the Stanley schools. The total number of pupils was 209, the largest class being thirty-two, and there were fourteen teachers. We started with the youngest class, the 5-year-olds, and went right up to eldest, but the headmaster said boys and girls did not necessarily leave on their fifteenth birthday. They usually stayed until they had a job, either as a shop assistant or in a clerical capacity in Stanley. They all wanted to stay in the town, or to leave the islands, but here the only outlet was as a seaman. There was a commercial class, but none in domestic subjects for the girls, although the boys had woodwork, and it was hoped to teach metalwork also. I was shown the woodwork-room and the laboratory. Both seemed fairly well equipped but, as all supplies came from Britain, the cost of apparatus was high. The head-master explained that out of the £1,500 pounds he was allowed for stationery, books, material and equipment, one-third went in freight charges. He had to compile an order from catalogues, and by the time it reached Britain prices had gone up so he never reached his full order.

There was a special class for backward readers. The teacher expected them to catch up with the others in two terms, their backwardness not being due to any mental defect but to cir-cumstances—usually they were Camp children sent to stay with Stanley relations so as to have the advantage of full-time day-school education. Such children often find it difficult to adjust themselves to urban life. They are slow in expressing themselves, lacking in imaginative thought and unable to co-operate even in play. Later I heard of a very extreme case. The little girl was the only child on an island farm, her playmates being dogs, and when she attended school in Stanley she began by going round on all fours and putting out her tongue like a dog. The lady who told me this story said she saw 'Mary Anne' a year later, and she had grown to behave like other children by then.

Attendance at the Stanley schools is excellent. The previous week it was 97 per cent, and I was told the figure did occasion-ally reach 99 per cent. I enquired about school meals, but there were none. Children whom the Medical Officer considered to be delicate had half a pint of milk free per day, but they had to bring their own mugs or cups to obtain it.

The annual prize-giving was held at the town hall on 19th December, and I took the opportunity of attending. There was certainly no lack of interest that day among Stanley parents. The Governor and Lady Haskard were welcomed by the head-master, who gave the usual type of address that is expected at prize-givings, drawing attention to new buildings, examination successes and extension of outside activities. The Governor replied and complimented the headmaster on introducing a vocational training scheme. He concluded by saying this would be the last time he and his wife could attend the prize-giving because they were due to leave the Colony before the next one. Lady Haskard then presented the prizes, each of the girls curtsying and the boys bowing to her.

I was sorry I could not get to the Darwin school. I had planned to do so in late February, but then I got a sailing in January, after it was too late to fix up the visit before Christmas. That was the long summer vacation and term did not begin again until the third week in February. I saw the building from Vinson's house, and I heard a good deal about it from parents, also Mr. Draycott gave me a prospectus. At the Stanley school, the headmaster introduced me to a member of his staff, a Mr. Trevelyan who was the newly-appointed head and would be starting his duties in the forthcoming term.

The school was built by the F.I.C. at a cost of £35,000 in 1952, a time when wool prices and profits were very high because of the Korean War. The Company financed it in the beginning, but now this is the concern of the Falkland Islands Government, who pays the F.I.C. a nominal ground rent. There are forty boarders, from all parts of the Camp, but children living in Goose Green attend as day pupils. The teachers are all qualified and recruited directly from Britain. Type of education is general—for pupils leave at 15—and covers English, general mathematics, history, geography, art, religious instruction, elementary science and domestic science. There are also classes in physical education, while games and sports have their usual importance. I read an account of the sports that took place on 6th December. The two seniors and the two juniors who gain most points are presented with silver medals, the medals and some minature shields being the gift of London woolbrokers, Jacomb and Hoare. No-one doubts the value of this school, but there are critics who consider it is wrongly placed. They say it should have been a boarding-house in Stanley, where Camp children could stay and attend the town schools, for transport problems would be no worse than at present and Camp children would benefit by urban surroundings. Opponents argue that Stanley would only develop in them a distaste for Camp life.

Four girls and six boys came on the December *Darwin* from Montevideo to their homes in Stanley for the long vacation. The education at this Uruguay school, a British institution, is of grammar-school standard and is, of course, given in English. This is the only way a Falkland Island child can get higher education, unless he or she is sent to England, and that means even longer separation from parents. As one mother said to me sadly, "I have had to lose my children." From Montevideo they can come home once a year, but from England not oftener than every second year. One man told me that he was at boarding school in Britain during the 1914–18 war, and did not see his parents for six years. It was even worse in the 1890s. Two girls were sent away, did not like England, and managed to stow away on a ship sailing to the Falkland Islands. After months at sea they turned up at Stanley, but their stern Victorian father sent them back to school on the next ship that left. They only had ten days between voyages.

Education was a subject with which I was fairly well acquainted; but I could only be taken round the medical services as an ignorant observer. Dr. Ashmore kindly met me one morning at the hospital and, with the acting matron, took me on a tour of wards, etc., answering my questions and explaining things in non-medical jargon.

The King Edward VII Memorial Hospital was built at the beginning of World War I and opened in May 1915. It replaced the Victoria Cottage Home, set up by Governor Allardyce (1904–15), this being the first hospital on the Falklands. Previously, sick seamen from visiting ships had to be lodged in boarding houses, where no proper nursing was available and charges were unreasonably high; and in the *Falkland Islands Magazine* for 1897 I came across a protest against such lack of facilities. "The absence of a Hospital for the sick and of an Infirmary for the aged and broken down is a cause of astonishment to all strangers who call into the Port." But Stanley had to wait another eighteen years for a proper hospital.

The Stanley K.E.M. Hospital has thirty-two beds. Not more than half were occupied when I went round, and the patients included a few geriatric cases. On that day it just happened there were no maternity ones, for all mothers, from Camp as well as Stanley, come to hospital to have their babies. There were two State Registered nurses, one State Enrolled, and five nursing auxilaries. There are four doctors on the islands—the Medical Officer of Health and one assistant in Stanley, one on East Falkland at Goose Green, and the other on West Falkland at Fox Bay. Weather often prevents the doctor from getting to a patient, but he can now receive urgent messages and give first-aid instructions over the radio. Before radio, a Camp woman told me, she remembered how someone on a farm had to climb to the highest point and light three fires, this being the signal that the doctor was wanted. He still uses a horse sometimes, but relies mostly on the Beaver or a Land-Rover.

In 1968 140 patients were admitted to the Hospital, and twenty-three were referred to consultants in the British Hospital in Montevideo. This is one of the drawbacks of isolation. The *Darwin* only sails from Stanley once a month, and although a few spare berths are kept until the last minute for serious urgent cases, yet if a person becomes desperately ill after her sailing, he or she cannot go for specialized treatment for nearly four weeks at least. Ordinary operations are performed by Dr. Ashmore at the K.E.M. Hospital, but, as he has no anaesthetist, spinal anaesthetics have to be given even for abdominal operations. As for visiting specialists, the last eye consultant came in 1959.

Clinics for out-patients are held at the hospital, and in 1968 2,814 patients were seen by Dr. Ashmore and his assistant. He also made domicilary visits. In 1967, there were twenty-one deaths in the colony, the largest number being caused by heart and circulatory diseases. £44,930 was spent that year on medical services. That includes dental treatment, there being a full-time dentist and one dental mechanic, who work at the hospital but also make Camp tours, trying to visit every settlement once a year.

In 1952 an old-age contributory pensions scheme was introduced, and in 1967 this was made compulsory for all males, and women in certain cases. There is also a non-contributory scheme which provides pensions "for old people who were excluded by reason of age from contributing to the Pensions Equalization Fund", so cannot benefit from the 1952 scheme. Poor relief is administered by the Stanley Town Council.

The only Trades Union is the Falkland Islands General Employees' Union, formed in 1943, that has now about 500 members and a full-time secretary. I went to see the secretary, Major Goss, he also being major of the Falkland Islands Defence Force, a voluntary territorial organization. He is, or was in 1969, a member of the Legislative Council.

In this pleasant office, Major Goss told me that during the union's existence, wages of labourers had been raised from 1s. 4d. an hour to 5s. 1d., and shepherds, who formerly had £8 a month, now get £37. That is in addition to the usual 'perks' on Camp of free house, free meat, etc.

He showed me the agreement that the Falkland Islands Employees' Union had negotiated with the Falkland Islands Sheep Owners' Association. It took effect on 1st October 1969, securing minimum basic wages for labourers, shepherds, mechanics etc., also, hours of work, overtime and special rates. According to Major Goss, relations between employers and employees were now very good, but he did not mention what they were previously like, and it was from another source that I learnt about a general strike in Stanley in 1946, a strike that was on the point of spreading to the Camp when a settlement was made. There was nothing I could find to read details of this—no back files of newspapers, so all I knew was based on hearsay. However, I certainly came across much underlying bitterness about the past among Campers and ex-Campers. Grievances were that they were 'kept down' formerly, that shepherds' cottages used to be little better than pigstyes, that education was shocking, with a visiting teacher for one week in half a year, and there were complaints about it still being impossible to buy land of one's own to start a small farm. I did visit two dozen settlements and the shepherds' houses that I saw were modern and comfortable, but of course poor ones may exist. I was told many did. Much has been done to improve educational facilities in the Camp, with the Darwin boarding-school and more visiting teachers so that a child has lessons for one week out of every three. As regards smaller, individually-owned sheep farms, I doubt if more of these would be a practical, economically-profitable, policy, even if present owners were prepared to sell, which they are not.

Originally the Crown owned all land on the Falklands, but as the colony developed and sheep farming became established, vast tracts were sold to any interested would-be settlers. Today, except for a handful of individual owners, farms are the properties of 'companies', who put in managers, possibly with overseers as well. A glance at a map showing boundaries gives the names of these corporate bodies: Packe Brothers, Bertrand and Felton, Dean Brothers, Anson and Luxton, Holmsted Blake, Pitaluga Bros., Cameron Ltd. and, by far the largest owner, the Falkland Islands Company. Size of farms is usually between 4,000 and 160,000 acres, whereas the average size of an English farm is 100 acres. On the Falklands a farm of 100,000 acres carries from 25,000 to 30,000 sheep. Total number of sheep on the islands is now in the region of 600,000, less than one-thousandth of the world's total supply. The figure used to be 800,000, but it has been reduced to avoid overgrazing. While I was there, the team of agricultural experts had been sent from Britain to advise on several matters, especially improvement of the pastures; but one manager told me this would be a disadvantage, not an advantage, for richer pasturage would spoil the soft quality of Falkland Islands wool. About 4¾ million pounds (over 2,000 tons) of wool is exported every year, and is shipped to Britain for sale on the London Wool Exchange. In 1968, the wool clip realized £810,839, and I read that, "This contributes valuably to the U.K. balance of trade through exports of finished products and re-export of wool." The writer was referring to countries like Japan, who are buying Falkland-produced wool from Britain.

The Falkland Islands Trading Company was formed to farm cattle and sheep on the islands, and to start commercial business there. When its charter was granted in 1852, it had already acquired nearly half of East Falkland from a Uruguayan merchant, S. F. Lafone. The first manager—who incidentally had been British consul in Montevideo and married Lafone's sister—arrived in July 1852. His first task was to arrange rough temporary accommodation, then choose a site for the Company's store, but by the end of the year he was joined by a storekeeper, some shepherds and other workers and their families, while the ship also brought additional sheep for improving stock. After twelve years of struggle, sheep farming by the F.I.C. began to show a profit. Now, in 1970, the Company produces about 45 per cent of the colony's wool, has a huge capital investment in the islands and subsidizes the shipping service between Stanley and Montevideo, as provided by the *Darwin*. For bringing wool clip to London, the F.I.C. charters the Danish vessel *A.E.S.* and collects freight charges from other firms that avail themselves of this means of transport. The F.I.C. is apparently not interested in the proposed air strip at Cape Pembroke, although on 28th April 1952, it did charter a flying-boat of Aquila Airways that flew from Southampton to Stanley, taking a week because it stopped overnight at Madeira, Dakar, Natal in Brazil, Rio de Janeiro and Montevideo. It carried mail and passengers, and made both outward and return journeys with a full load, but financially this proved very expensive, and such a venture has not been repeated.

The Falkland Islands Government and the Falkland Islands Company are the two giants of the islands, the one administering the law and providing social services, the other being the power behind the economy through wool production and export. Without the Company Falkland Islanders could no longer boast of their financial independence and declare, "We never go cap in hand to the British Government for aid." Kelpers wish to remain a British colony, but are proud they are not, and never have been, a grant-in-aid colony. In a letter to the *Observer* in 1969, the Company's London manager wrote that, although about £300,000 had been received since the war from the Colonial Development and Welfare Fund, yet the colony "has paid to the U.K. Exchequer five times as much from taxation on sheep farming profits".

The Falkland Islands Government issues its own currency notes of £5, £1 and 10s. denominations, the silver, nickel, and copper coins in use being the same as in Britain and issued in Britain. Although the halfpenny was abolished in Britain in 1969, and the half-crown ceased to be legal tender on 1st January 1970, both were still being used on the Falklands. The currency notes, I was surprised to note, were printed in Britain by De La Rue and not in Stanley.

Thanks to the Reverend Peter Millam, I was able to go to the printing works, housed in the Secretariat building and owned by Mr. Joe King. This master printer, who does mainly government work, took an immense amount of trouble in explaining everything to me as he conducted me round.

The works occupied four rooms. The first was a storeroom,

very full because the United Kingdom firm that supplies paper
will only accept a minimum order of 3 tons, and this gives Mr.
King sufficient stock for eight years. The cost, with freight
charges, is £350.

In the second room was a printing machine made in Otley,
Yorkshire, that Mr. King had to erect himself when it came out
and which he has to keep maintained. He had two older small
machines, one dating back to the last century and the other to
1921. In the third room, his staff of three, apprenticed and
taught the trade by him, were engaged on sorting some government leaflets just printed, also a set of brochures done for the
Cathedral. The latter were in connection with the Bishop
Stirling centenary.

Finally we went into the remaining room and here I was
shown a machine for casting type, also a furnace for melting down used type. Mr. King said a large supply of ingots
arrived with the machine. Then he demonstrated casting type
slugs on a Linotype 78 machine, the cleaning of moulds, and
how the metal after constant use could lose so much antimony
that it became too soft for use. I also watched the remelting
furnace at work and saw slugs reduced to molten metal, and
cast into ingots which were then cooled by water.

I had been over big, up-to-date printing works in Britain, but
never over a small one like this, and I found the visit very
interesting. It was also illuminating to see how printing was
carried out on the Falklands, but I did wish it could have been
extended to turning-out even a weekly newspaper. Until I came
to the islands I had never before realized the value of our British
Press. A newspaper would not only have provided current news,
national and local, but it would have been a permanent record
of facts, prevented the perpetual spread of rumours and specula-
tions, and, by printing letters from readers, have provided a
safety valve for grievances. Only by word of mouth can a Kelper
draw public attention to a complaint. True he can send a letter
to the Governor or Colonial Secretary, but this is not the same
as 'writing to the newspaper'.

IO

Round the Islands Collecting Wool

W H E N planning to visit the Falklands I had some correspondence with both the former Colonial Secrtary, then with Mr. Bound, who was Acting Colonial Secretary for a time. As I had said I wanted to see West as well as East Falkland, Mr. Bound booked for me on a trip the *Darwin* was due to make at the end of December. She went to a number of 'ports' to collect bales of wool clip that would later be transferred to the A.E.S. and taken by her to London. The settlements on the *Darwin's* 30th December itinerary were Speedwell Island, Port Stephens, Weddell Island, New Island, Chartres, Roy Cove, West Point Island, Carcass Island, Saunders Island, Pebble Island, Johnson's Harbour, Port Louis, and Green Patch—thirteen in all—and the trip would take from five to six days. It involved sailing right round the west and north coasts of West Falkland and the north of East Falkland, and when I measured the distance on the map, including the long inlets of Port Stephens and Chartres, I calculated it was not far short of 1,000 miles.

It was said to be a popular trip, a number of British wives going to see West Falkland, and I heard the maximum of forty passengers would be on board, but there were only twenty-eight. They included Roz Barnes; the Archdeacon and his wife; Monseigneur Ireland; a Mr. Dudley Cordery, representative of the Blue Star Line; two Royal Marines; and the F.I.C. Chief Accountant, Mr. Milne, and his wife. Monseigneur and the Archdeacon came to contact members of their respective churches and to hold services as required.

The *Darwin* and her predecessors have made these wool-collecting trips for seventy or eighty years, and once it would take five weeks to sail round. Before the advent of Beaver float-planes and radio telephone, the only way of getting to an island not on the ship's route was to make a fire of diddle dee at a point on the mainland (i.e. on East or West Falkland) nearest to that particular island as a signal. A traveller describing this procedure says, "On perceiving the smoke of the answering fire from the island, one repairs to the nearest shepherd's hut to await the arrival of the cutter—perhaps for a week." The same writer complained that cutters belonging to these smaller islands were usually "in an advanced state of rottenness".

I asked Willie about the 720 bales that *Darwin* was scheduled to collect and he explained that a large bale would contain 600 pounds of wool, but a small one, known as a 'dump' only had 400 pounds. Inside each bale is a rod by which prospective buyers at a wool auction can test the quality.

The call at Speedwell Island was brief and made during the night, but we spent several hours at Port Stephens, where, besides 150 bales, there was freight to be shipped and a horse who was induced to swim out, with a rope round him, and then hoisted aboard. Port Stephens, and the other settlements, were less attractive than on my previous trip, for there were signs of death about everywhere. I was wrong in thinking August was the month for killing. Rotting carcases were strewn over the ground and on fences hung sheepskins drying. It was a mild sunny afternoon at Port Stephens, the kind of day one could sit out—wearing a jacket, of course—only the difficulty was to find a spot not fouled with bones or manure or rusty petrol cans. The new cadet (i.e. deputy) manager, Mr. Peter Robertson, with wife and two small children, arrived on the *Darwin* at their new home. They had come from Argentina—I think from Buenos Aires—and I wondered how Mrs. Robertson would like her surroundings and the way of life. Her husband had been brought up on West Falkland, where his father used to be manager of one of the Fox Bay settlements.

We left Port Stephens at half-past five and reached Weddell Island in three hours. Darkness had fallen, but I could distinguish figures waiting on the jetty and was soon being welcomed by the Fergusons. Then Thelma, as manager's wife, entertained the whole party—twenty-four now, for we had left the Robertsons behind—to tea, coffee, drinks and cake. On my way to the 'Big House' I learnt that two quarks were nesting in one of the Chilean trees in the Ferguson garden, but though Teena took me to see the birds it was too dark to distinguish them properly and impossible to take a photograph. The visit was all too short. Punctually at 10 p.m. the *Darwin* hooter was shrieking for our return.

I was absolutely determined to see New Island, although it meant getting up at half-past five the next morning when the one and only launch journey would be made. New Island lies further out than Weddell, and its western and northern coasts have some spectacular high cliffs. The earliest mention of this island is in 1812, when a Captain Barnard anchored there when he was hunting seals in the brig *Nanina* of New York. On an 1840 map drawn by James Wyld it is called San Felipe Island. The present owner is a Mr. Davies, son of John James and Agnes Davies, who are mentioned in Eleanor Pettingill's book *Penguin Summer*, written just after the Pettingills (ornithologists) spent a month there in 1953.

Besides penguins, on New Island nests the black-browed albatross *(Diomedea melanophrys)*, whose snow-white plumage has patches of blackish-brown on tip of tail, on wings, etc. It is generally known on the Falklands as the mollymauk, and its eggs are still occasionally eaten. Someone in Stanley offered to boil one for me but I declined, not being adventurous enough to tackle any kind of egg but a hen's. The mollymauk's is so large that it has to be boiled for three-quarters of an hour and is served in a mug, not in the ordinary egg-cup. Great care has to be taken because the shell is very tender. I think mollymauk eggs were eaten on the Falklands much more seventy years ago, for, in an old number of the Cathedral magazine, I came across a recipe for using two of them in a pudding. According to the directions, you beat them up with a tablespoonful of cornflour, put the mixture in a well-greased cake tin, then cooked it "at a good steady heat for a few minutes", and ate the resulting pudding with plenty of sugar. The cooking time prescribed did not seem to me at all adequate.

During the mating season courting mollymauks 'dance', that is they advance, bow to one another, advance again, bow again, a sight I should love to have seen had there been the opportunity, but during this brief visit to New Island there was not even time to get to the mollymauks, whose ground was a long way off. I and Roz Barnes and a Mrs. Clifton, with her two schoolboy sons, did manage to cover the 2 miles to the penguin colonies. It was a dreadful scramble over tussac that I think had been cut down, leaving tough roots and sawn blades of grass in a sharp prickly condition. Wellington boots saved our legs from real injury, but bits found their way over the tops and were very uncomfortable. However, we got near enough to the penguins to take hurried photographs of them and also of an impressive pointed black crag, its shape and colour unlike anything I had previously seen on the Falklands. Then, fearful of the *Darwin* sailing without us, we made our way back. She was still visible out in the harbour, so we availed ourselves of Mrs. Davies' invitation to call at her house for a cup of tea. There we found the Archdeacon and his wife and several others, including the *Darwin* Mate, Mr. Jones. I could enjoy tea and Christmas cake with him there, knowing Captain Miller could not sail without him. It was a very jolly party, for our hostess was an extremely lively person, and I was sorry when we had to leave, sailing time being 7.30 a.m.

Mrs. Davies' husband, John James Davies, known as Jack, had died the previous August, and I read an account of him in the *Monthly Review*. He was born in 1893. His father worked in the F.I.C.'s sail loft in Stanley. Jack must have worked there too, then gone to the Camp, where he was first at Teal Inlet settlement, then at Fox Bay East. While still in his teens he acquired a cutter and supplied the Stanley dairies with tussac to feed their horses, obtaining this from Port William and later from Kidney Island. In the late 1920s he got employment with the Albermarle Sealing Co. as a seal catcher. Then he bought a small vessel and used it for bringing mutton from Camp to the Stanley butchery. Next he rented Hummock Island, then the Jasons', and in 1949 purchased New Island, where he began sheep farming in earnest; but he still kept his love of ships, and the wreck of one he had, *Protector III*, was visible in the harbour as we returned from viewing the penguins. To quote from the obituary account, "Jack collected small craft as enthusiastically as other men collect stamps." His career seems to me to express the combination of seafaring and sheep that the Falkland Islands signify.

While we were on our way from New Island to Chartres, Captain Miller received a radio message from his brother, the manager of Roy Cove, saying that if I cared to stay there for the night he would see I was taken by Land-Rover to the Blakes at Hill Cove—I could pick up the *Darwin* from there. I knew the two brothers' parents, Mr. and Mrs. Sydney Miller, who lived in Stanley and had been at Roy Cove for Christmas, and they must have told Simon how I had also been invited for a week to Hill Cove and reluctantly cancelled this when I arranged to sail for Britain mid-January. It was a kind thought. I gathered there was a track between Roy Cove and Hill Cove that made an overland journey possible. I was tempted to send a radio message of acceptance to Simon Miller, but on looking at the *Darwin* itinerary I found I should then miss Carcass Island, a place I was very eager to see, and so I kept to my original plan.

We sailed along the estuary of the River Chartres, but Captain Miller had to anchor some distance from the settlement, due to the shallowness of the water and the presence of sandbanks, so we had a forty-minute further trip by launch. I was charmed by the scenery on both sides—a line of rounded gentle green hills, their sides only slightly dotted with patches of diddle dee and bits of black rock, but there were several sprawling stone runs, the white of the quartz shining like silver in the sunlight. It was a lovely day and quite hot in the sun.

The jetty, like those on our previous calls, was crammed with bales of wool waiting to be loaded, and I had become quite used to clambering up one, then balancing and walking over the tops of the rest. Chartres looked a pleasant settlement, with plenty of green pastures and its still flowering gorse hedges neatly clipped, but there was the same charnel house atmosphere as at Port Stephens and New Island—I cannot speak for Weddell or Speedwell on this voyage for it was too dark for me to see them. I suppose it is the same with all settlements at this time of the year, but I did dislike the blood-stained sheepskins hanging on fences and the litter caused by bones thrown on the ground. Across the path from one house I saw a plinky, a kind of gibbet on which a dead sheep is strung up to be gutted. Killing of sheep on the settlements is done by slitting the throat. I saw green hay and oats being cut for fodder. They are the only crops grown and the climate does not allow them to be left to ripen. Horses and cattle are only kept for immediate farm needs, while the type of sheep is usually a crossbred with a strain of Romney Marsh.

Some passengers were claimed by friends and went with them. Some had not bothered to come ashore, preferring to sunbathe on the *Darwin* deck. The manager of Chartres, Mr. Bill Luxton, whose parents I also knew in Stanley, invited the rest of us to his house and—incredible as it may seem—the weather was so sunny and mild that we were able to have tea in the garden. New Year's Day will always remain in my memory as the day I did this unbelievable thing on the normally cold and wind-swept Falklands.

The Luxton garden was full of beautiful flowers, flowering shrubs, even a few shady trees, and a majestic white cat with weird black markings strolled across the lawn as we sat sunning ourselves in deck chairs. Bill Luxton said the temperature that afternoon was 71 degrees Fahrenheit—77 degrees being the highest ever recorded on the Falklands. After tea he took me round his vegetable garden, full of large lettuces such as I had not seen for months, and where he even grew melons and strawberries.

Finally he drove us back to the jetty, making two journeys as we were too many for one Land-Rover. Men were still rolling the last of his load of 100 bales, and as soon as the hundredth was put into a scow we chugged off in the launch, dragging both scows, the other being piled high with empty petrol drums, an old bedstead, and a couple of chairs. I was struck by the curious effect of heat on the hills that made a shadowy, ghostly outline behind the real contours.

It took two and a half hours to reach Roy Cove. Darkness had fallen before we got there, but I could dimly see both sides of the very narrow inlet, akin to a Norwegian fjord except for the hills being far lower in height, and I watched with awe as Captain Miller turned his 1,700-ton ship right round in the restricted space so as to face downstream. It was a clever piece of navigation.

Unloading the precious commodity, wood, at a West Falkland
settlement

Leaving Chartres in a launch towing two scows laden with cargo

The British Antarctic Survey ship, *John Briscoe*, at the public jetty
in Stanley. Kelp clings to its mooring rope

Friends being seen off from the Falkland Islands Company jetty on
the A.E.S. bound for London

The evening at Roy Cove manager's house was great fun. Simon Miller's mother, whom I already knew, was there, as well as his wife, and the brother, Captain Miller, soon joined us. 'Us' included Monseigneur and the Goulds, both Monseigneur and the Archdeacon reminiscing and making jokes about former visits. We did not leave until eleven o'clock, and I regretted that darkness prevented me from seeing the garden. I could dimly make out tall trees that Mrs. Sydney Miller said were planted twenty years ago, yet had reached quite a height. Roy Cove is one of the settlements noted for the good quality of its wool, and this usually realizes the best prices in the London wool auctions. It is about ninety years old. In 1887 there were fifty-three people living there and the settlement comprised several houses.

We had walked up the long, curving, rough, stony track that led from jetty to the 'Big House', and the way back would be easier because it was downhill, but Monseigneur had a lame leg and Simon Miller would not allow him to attempt it in the dark. I was prevailed on to make a third in the Land-Rover and was at first glad of the ride when I saw the others setting off, but I changed my mind when I found Simon's lights had failed, so he was obliged to steer with his left hand and illuminate the track by holding a lighted torch out of the window with his right. I felt like saying to Monseigneur, "This is when we pray," but did not dare. Anyway, we reached the *Darwin* without mishap, and later sailed for West Point Island.

I did intend to go ashore on this lovely island, of which Willie May had shown me transparencies, but we were actually leaving when I was awakened by Elie, the Uruguayan steward, bringing my coffee. Then it was a rush to have breakfast in order to catch the launch going to Carcass Island, for the two are not far distant. Here the water was so low that the jetty loomed high above us, and instead of stepping out there we had to walk underneath, which involved crawling over rocks covered with slippery kelp. Later I learnt that we were lucky to get to Carcass at all. If the wind had not veered round, it would not have been possible to get the launch sufficiently close. The owner, Mr. Cecil Bertrand, was waiting to greet us. He took us to his house where we were welcomed by his wife; also there, with her small daughter, was Heather May's sister Rose, whom I had met in Stanley and who had promised to look out for me. Her husband was one of the two shepherds, for Carcass is not a large farm and does not have more than 2,300 sheep.

Its history has been admirably given by Kitty Bertrand (Mrs. Cecil Bertrand) in an article published in the *Falkland Islands Journal* for 1968. Like so many islands in the Falkland group Carcass was first used by sealers as a base. Then in 1872, a Dane, Charles Hansen, obtained it on lease and began to bring in stock and to establish the settlement. I met a shepherd who had been on Carcass for twenty-two years and just left in order to return to his original home in the north of Scotland. He was travelling back to Britain on the A.E.S. Talking about Hansen, he said how he was an eye-witness of the tragic accident in which the owner met his death. There was a shed with a windmill to turn the dynamo for the electricity supply and Hansen, when trying out a new tractor, drove straight into it. The vehicle overturned and he was killed instantly.

In 1953 Hansen's widow sold the island to two men, Bertrand and Monk, but since then Mr. Monk has sold out and Carcass belongs exclusively to Cecil and Kitty Bertrand. Besides farming with up-to-date equipment and methods, they make a point of growing trees and shrubs for windbreaks and they encourage wild-life conservation. Sea elephants and jackass penguins breed on Carcass Island, and there is a rookery of the rare hair seal on two small islands near by, known as the Twins.

Carcass is a very attractive island and I did wish it had been possible for me to accept Mrs. Bertrand's invitation to stay for a weekend. I saw a sea elephant on the beach as we were coming up to the house, but could not get a photograph of him as he splashed into the sea on our approach. However I did get a good look at the quarks who had nests in trees in the Bertrand garden, for there were South American kinds and cabbage trees from New Zealand, as well as plenty of flowers, most growing outside but some in the entrance porch. I was particularly interested to find Mr. Bertrand had a Welsh grandmother who came from the famous Welsh colony of Chubut in Patagonia.

His wife is the daughter of a notable Kelper woman, Mrs. Napier, who died the previous September at the age of 81 and was the owner of West Point Island, now inherited by her son. In 1964, the A.E.S. was scheduled to call at Tristan da Cunha on leaving Stanley. Inhabitants of that remote island, 1,000 miles south of St. Helena, were evacuated to Britain when a volcano erupted, but later on the majority insisted on returning and a report was required as to how they were faring. Mrs. Napier heard this and, undaunted by her 76 years, was determined to see Tristan da Cunha, so she sailed on A.E.S. and, in spite of the difficulty of getting ashore, she managed to do so. I also read about Mrs. Napier in the *Sunday Express* for 24th November 1968, when Lord Chalfont was on his Falkland Islands 'mission' and landed by helicopter on Carcass. According to the *Express* the only person unable to be at the landing-ground was "eighty-one year old Mrs. Gladys Napier, who is too frail to leave her home". However Lord Chalfont called to see her and she made it very clear, in her usual vigorous manner, that the Falklands were to stay British.

Hill Cove was the last of the settlements on West Falkland that we visited. The manager, Mr. Tim Blake, met the *Darwin* and packed eight of us into his Land-Rover to see the 'forest', an experiment in tree planting carried out by his uncle forty-eight years ago and involving great care to ensure survival. Today it is a proper wood and shows what can be achieved, for though Hill Cove lies in a fairly sheltered creek the winds blow strongly and easily destroy tender shoots. The height and thickness of the trees was amazing. They were chiefly South American species, except for Austrian pines, and unknown to me, but their profusion and glory made me homesick for Britain, especially arousing a feeling of nostalgia for 'leafy Warwickshire', my native county.

We were entertained to tea at the Blakes' house. I had met Tim's wife, Sally, in Stanley when she came to have her first baby, and now I saw Paul again, as well as Sally's parents and aunt, who were staying with her. The return journey to the jetty was less crowded for Tim produced a second Land-Rover that one of our party drove. Again we sailed away, this time bound for two islands off the West Falkland coast, Saunders and Pebble.

Saunders is where the first British settlement of Port Egmont was set up in 1766, a year after Captain Byron planted the British flag there, but time was too short for me to ask Mr. Pole-Evans, the manager, to show me the site. We just managed a twenty-minute call at his house, where his wife was interested about my stay on Weddell Island, for Weddell, like Saunders, is owned by the firm John Hamilton Ltd., and has the same overseer, Mr. Robertson.

Weather changes with extraordinary rapidity on the Falklands. The day before had been phenomenally warm. That afternoon was sunny, windless, and still mild, though somewhat cooler; but on leaving Saunders Island in the early evening there was a bitter wind, and I felt frozen as I waited by the jetty for the launch. Such cold did not make me anxious to go ashore at Pebble Island, which we reached late that night and where we anchored. Loading was to begin at six next morning, but there were only fifty bales and I found there was no hope of reaching the other side of the island, where was a beach with sparkling, jewel-like pebbles, hence the name. These tiny stones sparkle and have been set into rings and brooches, but not locally. They were always done in England and the woman in the Stanley shop that was said to stock them told me people preferred the usual costume jewellery and she no longer bothered with having Pebble Island stones made up.

Our course was now set eastward and we had a sail of eleven hours along the northern coasts of West and East Falkland before we turned south and visited three settlements in Berkeley Sound. Nearly all the time we were out of sight of land, and the only excitement was the Eddystone Rock, which we were due to pass soon after midday. I have sailed by other isolated rocks but never by one so clumsy and ugly as this. It is named after the English Eddystone, though not having seen the latter I have no idea if there is any resemblance between the two. I should think not. Certainly no lighthouse could be built on this 260-feet-high lump of rock that I found described in a nautical manual as a "steep-to all round". The same book said from a distance of 8 miles it "resembles a vessel under sail". I thought it looked more like the ruined ventilating shaft of an old disused coal mine, or some other survival of Victorian industrialism. It rose out of the sea, straight and sheer, and, as far as I could see, the rounded top was bare of guano, so evidently no birds alighted there. We were about 4 miles from the coast, out of sight of land and with nothing to break the monotonous expanse of sea but this grim sentinel. I wondered if it could be a relic of the ancient submerged continent of Gondwanaland, or if, like the Falklands, it was a bit of Africa that had travelled westward in the far-off aeons of time. The Elizabethan adventurer, Sir Richard Hawkins, noticed it from his ship in 1594 and said it was "like to the Conduit-heads about the Citie of London", and the French explorer, Bougainville, called it Tour de Bissy.

To get a photograph I went on the lower deck, which was crammed with cargo, and found I had to clamber over a Land-Rover shipped from Pebble Island, avoid several sheep carcases and a dead upland goose, then make my way around two rowing boats—all before I could get to a suitable place for focusing the rock, and with the light just right.

During the afternoon we sat in the lounge and watched three films that Captain Miller had obtained from a settlement where they had been on loan. The Central Film Library was set up in Stanley in 1953 and now has a membership of eighteen settlements as well as the *Darwin*. For a subscription of £100 a year, it lends films to be shown in Camp community halls or on board ship. The first one that afternoon was an excellent documentary of the Falkland Islands, with shots of the kelp, of birds and sea lions, and it included a visit to Beauchêne Island that belongs to the Falkland group but lies 50 miles further south. It is covered with tussac, has many rare birds breeding there, including the albatross, but no human inhabitants, and has been designated as a nature reserve. Secondly we saw a film of a South Georgia expedition that followed in the tracks of a former one by Shackleton, and finally there was a drama of the Spanish Civil War.

Passing Volunteer Point on East Falkland, we sailed up the wide inlet of Berkeley Sound, making straight for Port Louis, the most historic place on the Falklands, for here a French nobleman, Antoine Louis de Bougainville, came seeking a new colonial territory for France to replace Canada that she had been forced to surrender to Britain. In February 1764 he came ashore with two refugee families from Nova Scotia and a crew of forty and immediately set them to work on building living accommodation and a fort. The only available material was peat sods and earth. Notwithstanding, a house and Fort St. Louis were finished in a few weeks, and the tiny settlement, that soon expanded, was called Port Louis. Three years later, France yielded to

Spanish pressure and withdrew. The Spaniards called the place Port Soledad, but when Britain took possession of the Falkland Islands in 1833 the name reverted back to Port Louis.

Driving me to his house, the manager, Mr. Grant, explained it incorporated part of the old British barracks, and he pointed out one wall where the original windows could be seen, though now blocked up. Inside he showed me the great thickness of the old walls. Mrs. Grant entertained us in the modern part, but, as he said, "You have been in the oldest house in the Falklands."

Not far away was the grave of Matthew Brisbane, the first superintendent of Port Louis, who was murdered by gauchos on 26th August 1833. There is a local legend about his faithful horse haunting the place, and two of our passengers declared they had seen the ghost. They were standing by the grave in the dark when they were chased by a horse, and nothing would convince them it was an earthly one.

Green Patch, where we called next morning, was a particularly pleasant settlement and lived up to its name. After Green Patch came our last port of call, Johnson's Harbour, named after a Dane who was known as Pirate Johnson. As a boy he was believed to be the only survivor of a party that buried treasure somewhere in Berkeley Sound. He left the Falklands, returned in 1841, and died twelve years later when he was in the early forties. The present owner and manager is a cousin of Peter Millam, the senior chaplain.

Roz Barnes and I were entertained to lunch by the Aikins, Jack Aikin being a cousin of Sid Barnes. The elder girl was a very enthusiastic horsewoman, and she explained to me the terms in use on the Falklands for horse harness and gear. They are nearly all Spanish ones, like *cincha* for girth and *maletas* for saddlebags, and go back to the early days of colonization when gauchos came from the South American mainland to handle the cattle and only left when sheep farming replaced the cattle business. The word *mañana* for tomorrow is still often used in Camp, as is the verb *pasear*, really meaning to walk but there meaning to go on a visit; while if you hobble a horse to keep it from straying you *mane* it. Hobbling is common on land where there are no trees.

Regarding horses on the Falklands, Willie May told me that

they were terrified of sea lions, even of the smell of a skin. He was once out riding with a couple of men on West Point Island and one had a piece of sea-lion skin in his pocket, but not one of them could manage their horses until it had been thrown away.

Jack Aikin went back to the ship to find out when Captain Miller was likely to sail and found it would not be until half-past one, so he and his wife insisted on us having lunch; another girl passenger who had come to claim a promised kitten was also invited. We were shown round the garden and introduced to two pet lambs for whom Eileen Aikin had rigged up an ingenious feeding contrivance, two bottles turned upside down and with the teats each protruding from a hole in the bottom of a wooden box, just the right height for the lambs to stand side by side sucking contentedly. Osmond, Peter's cousin, arrived and as I had heard he was knowledgeable about Falkland's history, I asked him about the elusive novel I was trying to trace, *An Island Princess*. He had never heard of it but said his great-uncle left him a collection of books that he had not yet properly examined. He did know, however, there was a diary kept by Great-Uncle from 1870 until his death and that it gave day-to-day details of the Port Louis sheep farm. It sounded a unique record that would be very helpful to any historian of Camp life.

Returning to the *Darwin*, we found the launch crowded with sheep carcases and dead upland geese. The kitten, held by her new mistress, was terrified until the wind sent whiffs of mutton and goose at us, and I saw her perk up as her little nose sniffed what to her was a delightful savour.

After reaching Stanley, the *Darwin* would start on Monday morning to unload her cargo of 750 wool bales; they would be be stored in the F.I.C. sheds prior to being put on the A.E.S. for London. A.E.S. was expected to arrive in two or three days, that is on 6th or 7th January, and sail out again about 14th January, with myself among the homeward-bound passengers. Meanwhile, *Darwin* had nine more settlement calls to make, seven from the 6th to 9th and two—to places I had already seen —on the 11th. There was an opportunity to see some fresh settlements if I took the next trip, so on the Monday morning I went to the F.I.C. office and booked.

There were fewer passengers. They included Captain Miller's wife and 6-year-old son, Jason, and a Mrs. Pirie with her little daughter, Maurag. Liz Pirie came to the Falklands as a nursing sister at the King Edward VII Memorial Hospital in Stanley, then married the full-time teacher of the Port Howard schools. Port Howard was our call on this trip, and Mrs. Pirie expected her husband, who was flying from Stanley, to be on the jetty there to greet her; but now a Beaver was stranded with engine trouble so flight schedules were delayed and she was beginning to think she and Maurag would be the first to arrive after all. Another passenger was Mrs. Gordon Johnston, wife of the E.S.R.O. chief, whom I had met at Government House on Christmas night, and she was bound for San Carlos to stay with her friend Mrs. Monk.

We sailed northwards along the East Falkland coast, making for the narrow channel leading to a wide expanse of water where there are several settlements: Rincon Grande (a reminder of the old Spanish influence in its name), Teal Inlet, Douglas Harbour and Salvador. Getting ashore at the last was even more of a feat than usual for the tide was very low and there was danger of the launch going aground, so she had to push the scows instead of pulling them and passengers walked along planks balanced on the scows, climbed a ladder and thus scrambled up to the jetty. Then followed more balancing as we walked over the bales. Loading the seventy would take three hours, we were told, because of difficult weather conditions.

Peter Millam asked me to return a book about missionary work in South America that he had borrowed from a shepherd at Salvador, a Mr. Davies. Peter needed it for the Bishop Stirling centenary since it gave a detailed account of the missionary bishop's work. I did not know this Mr. Davies, and Mrs. Johnston and the other two wanted me to come with them to call on the manager's wife, Mrs. Pitaluga, so I asked a lady who lived at the settlement if she would give the book to him, and she willingly consented. But, such is the prejudice against Argentina, she was very put out when she saw the book's title and found it concerned South America. She was most indignant and said she would not have handled the book if she had known it was about "Argies". In vain I pointed out it had nothing to do with present-day politics.

The manager's house was built nearly fifty years ago, but the Pitalugas had extended and modernized it, changing it from bungalow to a two-storey building, adding a charming sun parlour and putting in central heating. I understood small-bore pipes could not be used with peat, but Mrs. Pitaluga assured me that theirs ran perfectly with an electric pump. She had a beautifully equipped kitchen, with both Bendix and Hoover washing machines and plenty of cupboard units. In fact it was the sort of kitchen one never expected to see in such remote islands as the Falklands. As at Hill Cove, I admired the lovely modern pictures hanging on the walls. Then my hostess took me into the sun parlour, where she showed me her original collection of tiny cats, representing all breeds and made from a variety of materials, from china to soap.

Two passengers were leaving the ship at San Carlos, which, with Port San Carlos, lay on the west of East Falkland, and it took us most of the night to sail from Salvador waters to the San Carlos estuary. Here is another Spanish name, and it is believed that the Spaniards or the Argentinians had a penal settlement, supposed to have been situated at Bull Harbour, a place that is not shown on any existing map, but must have been on the estuary. In December 1831, an American corvette, the *Lexington*, reached Port Soledad (Port Louis) with instructions from the United States to sack the settlement to avenge the seizure of an American sealer. The Governor, Vernet, was denounced as a pirate and he managed to escape to Buenos Aires, while a temporary governor, Mestivier, avoided capture, but during 1832 he was killed by mutineers when sailing to the penal colony in San Carlos waters. The two modern sheep-farm settlements lie on either side, one at Careening Cove and the other on the eastern side of the southern bank, while into the estuary flows the San Carlos river that is navigable for small vessels for about 4 miles and for rowing boats another 2 miles. Rivers are rare in the Falklands and this one has an abundance of fish.

The other passenger leaving us, besides Mrs. Johnston, was a young man teaching at both settlements under the Voluntary Service Overseas scheme. He would be returning to England after a year's work to read for a degree in geography and economics at Reading University. It was interesting to talk to him, both about his own future plans and about his year's experience of life on the Falklands. He liked the Camp very much, but was not very enthusiastic about Stanley.

Mrs. Johnston went ashore immediately after breakfast. Mrs. Miller, Mrs. Pirie and myself were sitting chatting in the lounge when Captain Miller came in with Mr. Monk, the manager of San Carlos. I was introduced and included in his invitation to smoko. We were not leaving until seven o'clock that night because the *Darwin* had grounded owing to the lowness of the tide, a piece of information that did not worry me then but was to cause me much concern later. It was only during lunch at the Monks', when we were joined by Captain Miller, that Mr. Monk said, "Well, Nigel, I hope the *Darwin* is not stuck on my jetty for three weeks as she was once before." For a minute I thought it a joke, but after some noncommittal remark by Captain Miller, Mr. Monk added, "You won't get away until the wind changes, and that may not be for days. It is blowing you right against my jetty." I felt myself growing cold all over. This was 8th January, and there were only six days before the A.E.S. was due to sail, and if I missed her I should have to remain on the Falklands for another eight months because of the shipping congestion! True, one of the Beaver planes could come to fetch me into Stanley, but a Beaver could not land on San Carlos waters in a high wind, and the wind had been blowing gale force when we came off the *Darwin* earlier that morning. I supposed it might be possible to get overland, for San Carlos is on East Falkland, but with no roads and only occasional tracks and the treacherous peat bogs, I had no idea whether or not any owner of a Land-Rover could be induced to take me. As for riding on horseback, I should need a guide, and as I had not ridden for many years, I could imagine myself being carried on a stretcher aboard A.E.S., that is if I ever got there. It sounds ridiculous that a mere 50 miles should be such an obstacle, but such is the Falklands.

Anyway I tried to dismiss my worries and played with Jason and Maurag in the Monks' lovely sheltered garden, where there was even a croquet lawn. Then we four women chattered, had tea, and finally at half-past five there came a message that we must return to the ship. When we reached the jetty the wind was so awful that we had a frightful struggle walking along it.

The two small children, Jason and Maurag, were real champions and fought their way valiantly while we adults tried to shield them all we could.

For the next hour and a half I looked through the front windows of the *Darwin* lounge, watching the frantic efforts being made to get the big ship away, with the fierce wind driving her forward and Mr. Monk watching to see his jetty was not damaged. Captain Miller, the mate Mr. Jones, the second mate and, so it seemed to me, the entire crew were congregated up in the bows. I saw the two scows being put overboard. Once afloat they were lashed together, secured to the launch that was already there, and into them a derrick swung a long heavy cable, similar to the one attached to the anchor, which was of course down in the sea bed but not properly holding us. Then I realized that the anchor was on one side towards the stern and the plan was to operate the cable in the scows like a second anchor, thus dragging the ship away from the jetty. However, the wind was too strong. I watched Mr. Monk drive off in his Land-Rover, and Captain Miller and his crew abandon the effort for that night.

Operations were to be resumed early next morning. Everyone tried to reassure me that the F.I.C. would never let me miss the A.E.S. Beaver, or Land-Rover, or even the cargo ship *Forrest* would come to fetch me if we remained stuck indefinitely. In fact the Company began to sound like a fairy godmother! Of course, there was every hope the wind would change. Besides, I did not see how the A.E.S. could sail for England with only half her cargo. At least that how I tried to console myself as I swallowed a sleeping tablet and went to bed, trusting there would be an improvement next morning.

I was still in a drugged state when I woke and wondered if it was imagination or could I hear machinery working? Then I dozed off, woke again and looked out of the porthole, hardly daring to believe that the green hills opposite were different green hills from those of yesterday, but I was not certain. The scenery looked the same, I thought. I could not tell whether or not we were moving. Yes, I believed we were. Not able to bear the suspense any longer I flung on a dressing-gown and went to the lounge where the steward Lucho was busy sweeping.

"Are we away, Lucho?"

"Si, senorita."

I peered through one of the front windows and in front was water, no longer that hateful jetty, so I returned to bed; fell asleep again and was wakened by Elie with morning coffee.

"Are we moving?" I demanded. "Have we left San Carlos?" Elie smiled broadly, *"Si, si,* you catch A.E.S. all right."

We were now on our way to Port San Carlos, where there was no danger because the water was far deeper. In fact I heard at breakfast that Alan Miller, manager of Port San Carlos and another brother of the captain, had sent a radio message that morning to the *Darwin,* jokingly begging his brother to remember that his jetty was *not* built of concrete. Thanks to the R.T. our plight at San Carlos was known all over the islands.

Like Roy Cove this was again something of a family party. Jasper was very excited at the prospect of seeing his cousins again—Philip being also 6 years old, Rowan 4, and Kirstin eighteen months; and I wanted to meet Alan Miller's wife, Carol, whose invitation to stay there in March I first accepted, then had to turn down because of my earlier departure from the Falklands. She came out as a teacher on contract from England, married Alan Miller, and must have found it hard to adjust herself to Camp life for she was obviously an intellectual person. The walls of her lounge were literally lined with shelves full of books. Like other Camp wives she had a very busy life with three small children, housework and other chores—which, at present, included milking the cows because her husband was without a cowman, but she told me she did it by machine which was easier than by hand. Today she had prepared lunch for fourteen, eight of us off the *Darwin* and one of the 'Grassmen' who had been staying with the Millers and was now returning to Stanley by ship. He said the rumour was going round Stanley, so he heard from his colleagues by R.T., that the *Darwin* had not only stuck on the rocks at San Carlos but was a total wreck.

Mr. Davies came with us to have supper at the Pole-Evans' when we reached Port Howard, and, as Mr. Pirie had not yet arrived by Beaver, there was also an invitation for Mrs. Pirie and Maurag. Port Howard is on the eastern side of West Falkland, on Falkland Sound, and though the entrance to the harbour is narrow, it opens out within and the anchorage is good for large vessels like the *Darwin.* In the eighteenth century it used to be called Adair's Harbour. The sheep farm settlement was established in 1866, and was the first one on West Falkland. In 1887 forty-two people were living there.

I had seen some charming managers' houses, but that of Mr. Douglas Pole-Evans was really the most attractive of them all. A conservatory blazing with blooms ran along one side, with study and sitting-room windows opening on to it. The sitting-room had plenty of books and on a low table was strewn magazines like *Country Life* and *Blackwood's* that I had not seen anywhere else on the Falklands. Besides Mr. and Mrs. Pole-Evans and their daughter Susan, there were six of us from the *Darwin* and three guests staying in the house: Mr. and Mrs. Clements, the parents of Sally Blake of Hill Cove, and Mrs. Harding, sister of either Mr. or Mrs. Clements. Finally we were joined by Mrs. Pole-Evans Senior, who lived near by. She and her late husband were friends of Dr. John when he stayed on the Falklands in the nineteen-thirties, and the friendship had continued over the intervening years.

I was still on my quest for a copy of Theo Gift's novel, *An Island Princess* and thought Mrs. Pole-Evans Senior might know about it, but she did not. I asked about the book that mentioned her, and she lent me a copy. It was *Sailor at Sea*, the reminiscences of an Admiral Hickling, who devoted a chapter to the Falklands in World War I, when, as he said, Stanley was "our only coaling base . . . in the South Atlantic" and therefore of strategic importance. Women and children were at one period evacuated from Stanley and sent to various settlements. "To give such an order was one thing, but to disperse them round that desolate country in bitterly cold weather where the only transport was by packhorse or by sea was another." Orissa Pole-Evans was mentioned in connection with her work in receiving and helping evacuees.

The evening was indeed a delightful end to my travels around the Camp, and again I wished I had been able to accept the Pole-Evans' invitation to stay. We had a sumptuous supper. I have tried to refrain from commenting on all the delicious meals hostesses provided in Camp, but hospitality was on the most lavish and generous scale imaginable, and something I shall never forget.

II

Before Leaving the Falklands

WHEN I returned from the first wool-collecting trip, I found that the A.E.S. was shortly expected at Stanley, though so far no radio contact had been made with her. I heard the operator saying again and again, "Fleetwing calling, can you hear me, A.E.S.? What is your position?" Later that Monday morning it was established that she was 370 miles away and hoped to reach Stanley Tuesday evening.

On Tuesday morning Heather turned on her radio set while I was having breakfast and I listened to the familiar voice of Captain Svendsen talking to a representative of the F.I.C.

The Company man said, "We have 750 bales for you already and the *Darwin* will be back Friday with another 450. Then she goes to Fitzroy and Goose Green for 250 more. With luck, Captain, you should get away a week Wednesday on the fourteenth."

"What passengers have I got?"

"Twelve, we think, but three extra held by government booking have yet to be confirmed. There is a young baby and three small children and one dog as well. Have you any livestock aboard?"

"One dog, that is all."

"Well, Captain, if the weather holds you should have a calm run up Stanley Harbour. And you expect to be in at 9 p.m. tonight. Is that correct?"

"Eight-thirty p.m. if we keep up this speed of ten and a half knots."

"In that case, I must warn you, Captain, that the *Darwin* is alongside our jetty till nine, so you will have to wait until she goes. The *Biscoe* is at the public jetty. Now have you been in contact with the *Perla Dan?*"

So the conversation continued. Captain Svendsen ended by saying he would radio his latest position at four o'clock that afternoon, and he added in jocular tones that he hoped the Company would get its "great ship" out of the way so that he could go straight to the jetty, "for one of my passengers is very impatient to meet her husband. This is Mrs. Peebles, wife of Lieutenant-Commander Peebles, whom I brought here with other members of the hovercraft in October."

The R.T. is something I shall always remember about the Falklands. While I was on the first wool-collecting trip, Heather and Willie heard the invitation given me from Roy Cove, and my reason for declining because I did not want to miss seeing West Point and Carcass Islands. They were naturally disappointed I did not get ashore at West Point, where Heather's parents were living, but she was pleased I met her sister Rose again on Carcass.

Because of my decision to go on this next 450-bale-collecting trip, I had barely forty-eight hours in Stanley before returning to the *Darwin*—now so familiar that she seemed like a home from home—on Tuesday evening. The weather was perfect, mild, no wind, and the water in the harbour as smooth as glass. I stood on deck looking across to the opposite bank called the Camber, where, on the long slope of rising green ground, were picked out in white stone the huge letters forming names of some ships notable in the colony's history. *Protector* was an ice-patrol ship and succeeded by two others of the same name, number three being bought by the late Jack Davies of New Island—I had seen her hulk lying in the harbour there. Most famous was *Beagle*, on which Charles Darwin travelled when she surveyed the coast of South America from 1831 to 1836 and returned to England by way of Australia, New Zealand, Mauritius and St. Helena. She called twice at the Falklands.

This summer evening I gazed entranced at the lovely scene. Only near the ship was the pale-green water dotted with pieces of horrible kelp. Further away stretched this placid lake fringed by green slopes ornamented with these historical names, while on my left was a background of greyish-mauve hills, and on my right the picturesque Narrows leading to the open sea. I was thinking about Darwin and how that long voyage in the *Beagle* altered his conception of the universe and gave him ideas that caused him to write the world-shaking book, *The Origin of Species*. He only spent a few days on the Falkland Islands and took a violent dislike to them, using the damning descriptive adjective of "miserable" and saying they had a population (this was in 1833 and 1834) "of which rather more than half were runaway rebels and murderers". Two gauchos took him to see wild cattle, then roaming East Falkland, and, after killing a cow, he describes how a large piece was roasted on the embers of a fire "with the hide downwards and in the form of a saucer, so that none of the gravy is lost". He was surprised there were no trees, "although Tierra del Fuego is covered with one large forest," and he found the geological structure of the islands an interesting study, the first time that he began to respect geology as a science.

There were no birds that evening and the stillness was suddenly disturbed by a small launch and behind it a water-skier —yes, a man engaged on this incredible sport for a sea of low temperature, a sea that was seldom warm enough for the hardiest to bathe or swim in it. Round and round the harbour he dashed, and several others joined me to watch this unusual occurrence. One of the crew said the man was wearing a rubber suit to protect him from the cold. Another said he was recently back from 'the ice'—not that he could have indulged in water-skiing around Antarctica.

The display ended, and as I turned to leave the deck I heard a cry of, "Here is the A.E.S." She was just visible as she entered The Narrows, and the sight of her after three months was to me emotionally overpowering. Though a Danish ship, she was a tangible familiar symbol of Britain. She had come from London, and in less than a fortnight, in fact a week tomorrow if loading was finished, I should be aboard her and on my way to London. The way of a ship in the midst of the sea! At the end of The Narrows A.E.S. came into view again, after being hidden for a few minutes, and I thought her one of the loveliest and most inspiring sights I had ever seen. She was my link with Britain. Fascinating and beautiful as were the Falklands, and kind as many Kelpers had been to me, yet I did not belong to the islands. I had enjoyed my stay but now I wanted to return to where I did belong.

Darwin was now on the point of leaving, but A.E.S. had to wait until she pulled out. Meanwhile the hovercraft had come to welcome the lieutenant-commander's wife. There was a grand display of its powers as it went round and round and round the A.E.S., and this only ended as we moved away and A.E.S. started up her engines to come in and take Darwin's place. Congestion for berths is unsual. More often than not Stanley Harbour is empty of ships, but the following Sunday there were five, a record number. Against the F.I.C. jetty, side by side, were A.E.S. and Darwin, and I had to climb from one to the other when disembarking on my return from the second wool-collecting voyage. The government-owned Forrest was at the government jetty, and B.A.S. Perla Dan at the public jetty, and anchored in the middle of the harbour was the other B.A.S. ship John Biscoe.

British Antarctic Survey headquarters were set up in Stanley in 1950, and their ships are used to take supplies and personnel to the Antarctic bases at Halley Bay, Marguerite Bay, Signy Island etc and now to the recently-acquired one at South Georgia. Extracts from a newsletter by the officer-in-charge were published in the February 1970 Monthly Review, and he reported then, about a fortnight later, when both vessels had left Stanley on their routine voyages, that Perla Dan was well down into the Weddell Sea. "Ice conditions met have not been too bad, indeed only one bad patch of ice has been encountered so far. Satellite photographs show, however, that ahead of her lies a fair amount of coastal pack. The John Biscoe, having met pack after leaving Argentine Islands, is now lying some 100 miles to the west of Marguerite awaiting better visibility and an aircraft reconnaissance of ice conditions along the approaches."

It is amazing how the ice grips a man, how the two cold inhospitable regions of the earth capture his imagination and lure him to visit and revisit polar lands. When he has been as far south as South Georgia he feels he is a creature apart—though that island, not being within the Antarctic Circle, does not give him the distinction of being allowed to put both feet on the dinner table while the port is circulated. (Years ago this was established as the privilege to men who had crossed the

Circle.) Those who had rounded Cape Horn could put up one foot only. I heard of a B.A.S. man who, when he arrived at a base, declared he could never stick life there even for a limited period and he refused to go ashore, but at last he was persuaded to do that because the ship would not leave for a fortnight. During those two weeks he grew so attached to 'the ice' that he remained for fifteen years, renewing his contract twice and willing to do it for a third term, but as he was at retiring age B.A.S. would not permit it.

Friends of the Mays were Russell and 'Tricia Johnson, Russell being a government meteorologist, working on the Falklands for a second term, and under both B.A.S. and the Falkland Islands government. The couple often came to spend an evening with Heather and Willie, or we went to their delightful modern bungalow in Ross Road, and I found them both lively and interesting, exceptionally so for Stanley. On one occasion they brought with them a young airman who was going to Adelaide Island, just within the Antarctic Circle, near Marguerite Bay in Graham Land, that stretches for hundreds of miles up the northern tip of Antarctica. He was sailing there on the *John Biscoe*, but on his return he had to pilot a plane from Adelaide Island to Punta Arenas over what he said was the worst sea in the world. It was no use having floats on a plane, or bothering with life-saving jackets, for if you were unfortunate enough to come down you would not last five minutes in those waters.

Russell was interested in my book. In fact his usual opening question was, "Have you finished it yet?" In vain I explained I had not written a word because I first had to collect information, then sort it, and such a dilatory method appeared to him quite mad. Concerning the collection of information, he offered to show me round the meteorological office and explain its workings to me, and when he did he took a great deal of trouble to clarify everything as far as possible. There were two offices in Stanley, first the colony forecasting service, secondly the British Antarctic meteorological service. The office of number two was staffed by a qualified officer and two technical assistants, and was occupied with collating reports from the B.A.S. bases about weather there.

The colony forecasting department, staffed by two, reported normal meteorological data, such as temperature, pressure, cloud, wind, sunshine and rainfall. Russell showed me the equipment, all installed out of doors. A perishing wind was blowing that morning. I once attended some astronomy lectures and was surprised to learn what uncomfortable times astronomers had looking at the heavens in bitter cold, for no heating is possible in an observatory or it would spoil telescope reception. Meteorologists are also martyrs to their work. Every day, or several times a day, Russell would check readings on his instruments. I viewed one set in damp grass and reached another by climbing up a ladder to an exposed windswept platform, where a glass ball recorded sunshine and Russell said that even in winter it was rare to have more than three sunless days. Information obtained, together with observations from B.A.S. bases, was transmitted by radio-telephone printer and Morse to other countries in the southern hemisphere.

The problem of weather is particularly important in this part of the world. If storms are forecast, the meteorologist wants to know in which direction and how far they are travelling; whether they are likely to increase in violence or to die out; and what kind of weather they will bring to the Falklands. Three special characteristics mark the physical conditions of the islands. They are in the path of strong westerly winds coming from polar regions; the land is covered by peat bogs and small lakes; there is not an excessive amount of rain.

Before I left, Russell listed for me other observations that were taken in Stanley. There was solar radiation; the sampling of carbon dioxide, done for Glasgow University; the sampling of rainwater and nuclear fall-out, results being sent to Vienna, to Copenhagen and to Harwell.

Then I looked at a report, published in 1920 by C. E. P. Brooks on *Climate and Weather of the Falkland Islands*. It was historically interesting to me. It stated that the first to do any weather work was Sir James Ross, who recorded in *Voyage to the Southern Seas* his observations from April to August 1842; and that regular records were kept near Stanley at the Cape Pembroke lighthouse from 1850 onwards, being rather poor at first but first-class after 1903.

Also beyond my range of knowledge but explained to me as simply as was humanly possible was the E.S.R.O. station— really two at Stanley. There is the Satellite Tracking Station and the Ionisphere Wave Transmitting station. Both are under the control of Mr. Gordon Johnston, whom I first met at Government House on Christmas night and whose wife I saw again when we travelled together on the *Darwin* as far as San Carlos. They were among the very few Britishers who were really happy on the Falklands. Mr. Johnston rejoiced in being out of the rush and rat-race of contemporary England, feeling one could get on with the job without frustration in these islands, while he enjoyed the open-air life and was able to indulge in his favourite sports of golfing and angling. Mrs. Johnston too liked her environment immensely. I wished there had been an opportunity to know them better, for their outlook was different from that of many people I did meet. At least, I mean people in Stanley. Stanley and the Camp are like two separate worlds.

First Mr. Johnston explained about the Ionisphere Wave Transmitting station, which is one of 150 with headquarters at Slough in Buckinghamshire. Its function is to get the best wave transmissions, and Stanley is a station fitted with apparatus for studying radio waves coming from satellites.

We then drove through Stanley and out to Moody Brook, where has been built a satellite-tracking station that is part of the organization known as European Space Research, founded in 1965. It was agreed to put up four stations on a north-to-south line right down the globe, and Stanley was one of the selected places. It has a staff of twenty-two—all men on contract—and there is a direct telephone link with Slough and with the E.S.R.O. station in Germany.

Different kinds of equipment were shown me—antennae, receivers, pointing data recorder, 'quick look', and others just as mysterious and complicated. I did my best to grasp the function of each. For example, 'quick look' transmits temperature data from a satellite, while another machine counts the drift in micro-seconds, that is millionths of seconds. One device sent out instructions to robots in space. Information received back at the station was punched in a code pattern of holes on magnetic tape, and I watched the rapid decoding of data, for one of the Stanley station's functions is to collect these from satellites, the other two being the sending out of orders and the actual tracking. Satellites are identified by long numbers, each beginning with the last two numerals of the launching year.

A satellite passed over Stanley while I was in the E.S.R.O. building and it was almost as exciting as being in the Cape Kennedy control room during launching of a moon rocket. I watched green and red lights flashing on the appropriate machines. Men were observing them, but the machines did the vital work. They produced the essential information and they ceased to operate when the satellite had gone beyond the sky above the Falklands.

I was a day later than I expected in returning from my final *Darwin* trip, due to the delay at San Carlos, a delay that frightened and worried me out of all proportion to the situation. I really was scared of not being able to catch the January A.E.S. and being stranded on the Falklands for several more months. Looking back, this agitation sounds ridiculous, but with the shipping congestion it was a definite possibility. I met a man from Wales whose contract was just finishing but who could not get a *Darwin* passage until September and was taking a temporary job in Stanley to keep himself until then. Peter Millam's contract ended in May, and a few months ago he found there were no vacancies on the June ship, and no two-berth cabins on the July, but he did secure a four-berth one for himself, Jill and the two children on the latter. Talking to Des Peck of the Philomel Stores, I learnt he was taking his wife to England for a holiday in 1971 and had already booked accommodation for them in the April *Darwin*, fourteen months ahead. I was not the only person who developed a feeling of claustrophobia. Several temporary British residents were the same, and one often heard the remark, "When I get through The Narrows." It was like Lewis Carroll's Alice, going and coming back through the looking-glass. Certainly I had been backwards and forwards from inner to outer harbour on my three *Darwin* trips and when I went to Kidney Island, and, as *Darwin* sailed along the narrow dividing channel, that drawbridge to the castle, on the return from Port Howard on 10th January, I thought, "Next time will be the last, for then I shall be homeward bound."

A.E.S. was alongside the Company jetty and we drew right beside her, so that planks had to be placed for passengers to cross from one ship to the other, and thus get ashore. Two of the *Darwin* crew helped me to climb on to the plank. Balancing myself, I walked to the other end where two more were waiting on A.E.S. to assist me in the jump down to her deck. My case was thrown after me. I picked it up, thrilled to find myself once more on this dear familiar ship that had brought me over 8,000 miles from London and was soon to take me back there, and as I walked round the great hold, dodging cargo, Captain Svendsen appeared to greet me.

"Hello, Miss Taylor. Let me take your case. So pleased to have you on this voyage. You and Mrs. Barnes are sharing the owner's cabin, and you will be very comfortable there. But, alas, Kelly is not with us this time. He is on holiday at his home in Denmark. Let me introduce you to the Chief Steward who is taking his place."

On the following Monday and Tuesday, I made good-bye calls on people in Stanley who had entertained me, including the Bartons, the Millers and the Luxtons. I also tried to buy souvenirs to take back to friends in Britain, but all I could get were ash trays, either decorated with the Falkland Islands crest or a map, and both were heavy in weight. As I have already explained brooches and rings were no longer made with Pebble Island stones set in them. Years ago when I went to Iceland I returned with a sheepskin rug. I came back from St. Helena with one. Naturally I expected to buy at least two on islands where sheep farming was the only industry—but nothing of the sort! Heather had two very attractive rugs made from West Point Island sheep, black and russet, the one colour being naturally black wool and the other white wool dyed with crushed kelp, but she had them cured and made up at Montevideo. In the *Monthly Review* for the previous August, I read an account of the 1969 Winter Show, where exhibits included hand-made horse gear and horn work, articles knitted from home-spun wool, and local paintings, but it appeared that none were obtainable on sale. All I could have got were some black-and-white photographs that were being sold at the Catholic Bazaar, but I did not want them when I had my own cameras, one for coloured transparencies and one for black-and-white pictures.

The Secretary of the Guild of Spinners, Weavers, and Dyers, Wyn Hardy, used to come to Deanery coffee mornings, and I asked her if I might attend a meeting, which I did and was welcomed by Wyn and three other members, one of them giving a spinning demonstration for my benefit. There were ten spinning wheels, and the Guild was trying to interest schoolgirls through competition for a Mrs. Nancy Blackie prize, but it was admitted that not many were interested in the craft, and there was even less enthusiasm among young women of Stanley. In the Camp, it is better, so let us hope the guild does not cease to function through lack of support.

On the last Tuesday evening, Roz Barnes and I entertained Jill Millam, Asta Gould and Margaret Owen to dinner at the 'Upland Goose', something unprecedented in Stanley, though now I imagine it happens quite frequently. Over the Box, Mrs. King announced that the hotel would commence catering for small dinner parties at the end of January. However, as we were leaving mid-month, I went to see her and she agreed to have us, and she provided a first-class four-course meal, with roasted upland goose as the main dish at my special request. We five had a small dining-room to ourselves, and, with a delicious dinner and the accompaniment of good wine, the atmosphere was one of sophisticated luxury normally absent on the Falklands, and I grew even more impatient to return to a way of life less stark and grim than that of this most southerly capital in the world.

By this time I was sick of slopping around in slacks and padded jacket to keep out the chilly summer wind. My hair looked dreadful. It was a little better after Heather gave me a home perm, but with no trained hairdresser on the islands I could not have it cut, so it now had five months' growth and was too long and too thick to suit me. When I bought a white jacket, I did not realize how dirty that would get from peat dust and from scrambling about in cargo boats, but to have it washed would ruin the quilted lining and destroy its warmth, while there was no dry cleaner nearer than Montevideo. I doubt if anyone bothered to send clothes the 1,000-mile journey. It was the same with shoes. There was no way of having them repaired on the Falklands, unless you did them yourself, and I was no amateur cobbler. When, on my way to Britain, I examined the two pairs I had worn through on stony tracks, I decided they were too far gone to be worth bothering with, so flung them overboard. As for the grubby jacket, I did take that home and send it to a local cleaners from where it was returned looking as white as when I bought it.

Because of the delay at San Carlos, there was no chance of A.E.S. sailing until after the fourteenth, but she was expected to leave a day later. On Tuesday evening *Darwin* returned from Fitzroy and Goose Green and was able to occupy the public jetty, as the B.A.S. ship that had been tied up there had left for Antarctica. *Darwin* was due to leave for Montevideo on the sixteenth, and Dudley Cordery, the Blue Star representative, invited me to the farewell cocktail party he was giving on board the night before. I could only accept provisionally. All depended on whether A.E.S. went that afternoon or not, and in the end she did, at half-past three on 15th January.

But her sailing was in doubt until a few hours beforehand. All the time I had been on the Falklands there had been very little rain, certainly by comparison with the part of South Wales where I lived, but on that Wednesday heavy rain fell and all loading stopped. If bales of wool were put into a ship's hold in a damp condition, there was the danger of combustion, so, though a light shower did not signify, any real downpour meant cessation of work until the sun came out again. I was told that there might be a prolonged spell of bad weather now the fine weather seemed to have broken. A.E.S. might easily be delayed for another week before the loading of her principal item of cargo, the wool clip, could be finished, and passengers who had travelled from the Camp had to continue to stay in Stanley with relatives and friends. I was fortunate that the spare room at the Mays' was free. Of course I packed all my luggage except an overnight case, and was glad I had when Thursday morning was fine, but later there were a couple of showers and it was doubtful whether or not they might increase in severity as the day wore on. From the window in Heather's sitting-room, I could see that the A.E.S. derricks were moving to and fro, so loading was in progress—that of the last 250 bales brought from Fitzroy and Goose Green. At half-past twelve, the shipping clerk at the F.I.C. office phoned to say sailing time was fixed for half-past three that afternoon, and would I be on board by three o'clock at the latest. Announcements were also made over the Box.

Willie and Heather drove me to the jetty, and I had two passes for them to be admitted on board. Vivienne Perkins drove up with Roz and Joan Goodman, and the six of us had hardly collected in the very superior Owner's cabin, next to the Captain's quarters on the middle deck, when the Millams and their two children arrived, followed by Elwyn and Margaret Owen and their two babies. Margaret had sweets and magazines for us, while Peter Millam, amid much laughter, gave Roz and me each a large "Chad Valley Cuddly Toy" penguin—a gentoo with bright orange beak and feet. Then a steward came to say a Mr. and Mrs. Lee were waiting at the jetty gate, but were not allowed further because they had not got passes, so of course Roz and I had to leave our guests for five minutes while we ran across gangway and jetty to the gate and said goodbye—through bars—to kind Alf and Elsie, fellow passengers on the outward voyage. They had brought us a large tin of biscuits.

Someone made a joke about A.E.S. leaving with visitors still on board, and this alarmed five-year-old Kevin Millam. He was quite thrilled at the prospect of going to England in July, but he considered January much too soon, especially without luggage, so he was anxious to get off this ship before he was carried away from Stanley. Rosalind, with the superiority of eight years, had full confidence in her father's ability to prevent such a catastrophe, and had no patience with Kevin tugging at his mother's coat and suggesting they left. However, it was getting near sailing time, so our well wishers trooped down the companionway and over the gangway, while Roz and I stationed ourselves on the lower deck to wave *au revoir*. Other passengers were there as well, and I saw the Chief Engineer whom I knew from the outward voyage.

With the gangway removed, we began to leave the jetty. Someone was playing the bagpipes. Among the crowd I saw Elie, the Uruguayan steward of the *Darwin* and Jerry Moran from Aberdare, South Wales. Both waved to me, as did the friends who had come to see me off. Even at that moment I thought how ensconced in thick clothing everyone was, including the children, although it was summer. Kevin had a blue poncho, a South American knitted shawl with hole for the head to slip through and very popular among Stanley youngsters. Rosalind wore a bright red one, the colour contrasting vividly with Peter's clerical black, and behind them was a 10-foot pile of drums full of petrol brought from England by A.E.S. Now she was laden, not just with ordinary freight, but with a thousand tons of wool clip for the London auctions.

She turned slowly as she pulled away from the jetty, and I saw *Darwin* at the other jetty, Ross Road running parallel with the long line of harbour, and the conspicuous red-brick Cathedral. A.E.S. was heading straight for The Narrows, and on my right were the red, blue, and yellow roofs of houses stretching up the hill. Now we were passing the rubbish dump, now the cemetery, now bare green stone-studded country, land receding further away as we sailed through the great outer harbour.

I saw the *Great Britain* still rusting away in Sparrow Cove. A few months later a remarkable salvage operation was carried out and Brunel's masterpiece was towed back to Britain. Huge crowds watched her triumphal passage up the Avon to the dock from where she had been launched in 1843, and her return 127 years later was timed for the anniversary of that launching date, 19th July. Now this first iron-built ship, also the first to be driven by a screw propeller, waits for restoration, or partial restoration, to her former splendour.

12

Thirty-one Days on the Atlantic Ocean

ON the voyage from London to Stanley, A.E.S. took on sufficient fuel to last her for the return voyage so she was not calling
anywhere on the way back. When I went aboard on 15th
January, I knew I should not set foot on land for four weeks,
not until the evening on 12th February, and not so soon as
that if bad weather delayed us.

However, we started off with a calm sea and southerly wind,
thus making good progress, and when I came down to breakfast
next morning I learnt we were already 200 miles on the way
north. The A.E.S. dining-room had four tables, each holding
four or five people. At the captain's table was a place for the
chief engineer, who seldom appeared, and the remaining seats
were allocated to the two passengers sharing the owner's cabin.
On the way out Lieutenant-Commander Peebles and Lieutenant
Glennie sat there. Now it was Roz Barnes and myself. Not that
the captain's table was remote from the rest of the passengers
in space or spirit. The dining-room was small and A.E.S. was a
democratic friendly ship, so once ordinary strangeness was over-
come we chatted across to each other as we had done on the
previous voyage.

One table was occupied by a former chief engineer of the
Darwin, who was returning to his native Scotland, and by two
members of the Falkland Islands Police Force with a man they
were escorting back to London. This man had served two out of
a three-year sentence in Stanley when his health began to suffer
and he was now bound for England to receive treatment there.
I hope he has recovered. As far as we other passengers were concerned he was just another passenger, and as his escorts did not
wear uniform any 'guarding' was not obvious.

At the third table were Mr. and Mrs. Peck and their three little girls, aged 5, 4 and eighteen months, also Mrs. Jennings (Kathie) who had a baby only two months old. All three adults held British passports so did not come under immigration restrictions applying to those with Falkland Islands passports. The Pecks were moving back to Britain and he hoped to get an engineering job, for though he had been some years on a sheep farm yet prior to that he was at sea, as was Kathie Jennings' husband. She and her mother-in-law, Mrs. D. I. Jennings, were both bound for the Shetlands. Kathie's home was there and Mrs. Jennings had a daughter in Lerwick with whom she would stay until August. She sat at the fourth table with Colin and Richard. Colin had worked for twenty-two years on Carcass Island as a shepherd but was settling in the north of Scotland, his original home. Richard was really a commercial photographer who had been in various parts of the world, up north in Scandinavia and south in Bechuanaland. Some whim took him to the Falklands where he too had been a shepherd on a couple of farms, but he disliked the life there and was glad to be leaving, although he admitted the experience had been worth while. He would not be long in England as he was due to leave for the U.S.A. in April on an advertising assignment in Los Angeles. We had met before at a Deanery coffee morning when he was staying in Stanley prior to sailing.

Then there was the livestock, consisting of one bird and one dog. The bird, a linnet, belonged to the new Chief Steward, and it trilled from its cage outside his cabin until it escaped and flew out to sea where it would certainly perish. The dog was a miniature white poodle belonging to one of the former colonial officials on South Georgia. Mr. and Mrs. Quigley left with the administrator and his staff in December, but they were touring South and North America *en route* for England so the poodle had to be sent on the A.E.S., and, of course, he would have to go into quarantine on arrival. We could never remember his proper name and called him Quigley after his master. Not that he cared. For the first few days he was a miserable little creature. Then he became devoted to the cook, who made a great fuss of him and Quigley even slept on the cook's bed, but though he strolled into dining-room at mealtimes he refused all titbits and remained aloof and uninterested in us.

On the second day it was warm enough to sit on a deck chair outside, and at the end of the first week, with temperatures soaring into the eighties, the small canvas swimming bath was erected. It took me fully a week to recover from the exhausted mental state I had lapsed into after leaving Stanley—due, I think, to change of air. The air on the Falklands was almost overpowering in its freshness and strength. I must have missed this and could not easily accustom myself to much higher temperatures and the absence of wind. Most of that first week I felt too stupid to talk, even at mealtimes, and I spent whole days lounging in a deck chair, pondering about the elusiveness of the Falkland Islands and despairing of ever writing a book about them. Only as we approached Britain did the urge to write return and I knew I had at any rate to try and describe those baffling islands.

For I had found them baffling and elusive, but they were beautiful and unique as well. I was fascinated by the smooth bare hills, the soft pastel colours, the starkness of moorland, peat bogs and quartz outcrops, and the amazing richness of the bird life. They are indeed a revelation to bird enthusiasts, so much so that the only serious attempt at creating tourism has been for ornithologists, with the result that Kelpers cannot conceive of anything else interesting a visitor. As for the Kelpers themselves, their outlook still eluded me, but perhaps that was my own fault, although I could not see how it was I failed. Certainly I went to the Falklands prepared to accept and to understand, but I just could not penetrate a built-in reserve. Now, basking in sunshine on the A.E.S., I gazed for hours on end at the seemingly boundless ocean and tried to sort out my impressions and come to tangible conclusions. With the distance between myself and the islands increasing I could feel more detached, something that was impossible when I was actually there. Lawrence Durrell says that every land has "hidden magnetic fields" which only touch a traveller's own personality if he tunes in properly. I think I made the initial mistake of forgetting that any islanders are inclined to live in a world of their own, and that the remoteness of the Falklands intensified this tendency. Eight thousand miles separate them from Britain, and, without an airport, communications are virtually the same as they were seventy years ago.

Before I journeyed south, a former Stanley senior chaplain, the Reverend Eric Thornley, said to me, "It is impossible to convey on impression of life on the Falklands. You have to make a long stay, and either you hate the isolation or you love it." At first I did not hate it, but towards the end of my stay I did, and I suffered from feelings of being cut-off and shut in. Going through The Narrows on A.E.S. on 15th January made me liken myself to a spaceman re-entering earth's atmosphere after a moon flight.

Way of life on the Falklands appears complex to the outsider because of its dualism. Homes are modern, well furnished, and equipped with up-to-date, labour-saving gadgets. Yet there are outmoded social distinctions; there are underlying resentments that can find no proper outlet because of the absence of a daily or weekly local press; and, above all, isolation and the lack of mental stimulation cuts off Kelpers from the rest of the world. In Britain criticism is often levelled against television, but the introduction of such mass media entertainment in Stanley—and surely it could be done by satellite?—would bring a beneficial awareness of what goes on elsewhere.

I do not agree with one writer who condemned the atmosphere of the Falklands as completely early nineteenth century, but development has been sorely hindered by poor communications. A Stanley shopkeeper told me that the last thing he wanted was to have "the Argies over us", but that the Falkland Islands did need an air strip. He repeated the current rumour that Argentina had offered to build one at Cape Pembroke and he was dead against acceptance of such an offer because it would give the Argentine Republic a footing in what she regards as her Malvinas. But he concluded, "This place has gone backwards during the last twenty years because we are so isolated. I have seen it happen."

This time we had a different chief steward on the ship and I did not enjoy his catering as much as Kelly's. Bacon was only served for Sunday breakfast. At dinner sausages made their appearance far too often, sometimes floating in the soup and sometimes served with dishes of curry powder and curry sauce as the main course. There was one horrible soup that we had at least twice a week. It was like cold custard, and was, I suppose, a Danish recipe, but some Danish soups, especially one with sauerkraut, were delicious. Supper was cold meats, tinned fish, slices of boiled egg, beetroot, cucumber and dishes of pickle, but, as I have always found in Scandinavia, the assortment—exciting though it is at first—becomes monotonous after a time.

The chief mate, who came from the Faroe Islands, and the chief engineer, a Dane, were the same as on the outward voyage, and so was the second engineer, an Hungarian refugee. For the first engineer, another Dane, this was his first experience of the A.E.S. He was flown to Las Palmas to join her. Evidently this was because of an emergency, but his English was not good enough for me to make him understand my question, though he complimented me, saying, "You speak slow and clear so I understand what you say." That was on a later occasion and perhaps he had got more accustomed to my voice, or I made a deliberate effort to talk very slowly. He hated such a long voyage. "This is my last time. I go mad if I stay for another journey like this. The chief engineer, fourteen years he go backwards and forwards, backwards and forwards, London to Stanley, Stanley to London. How can he? Fourteen years, four times a year! Not for me! I tell you another journey like this drive me mad."

Some members of the crew came from Latin American countries—not Argentina, but Chile, Uruguay and Brazil, and the chief mate was trying to learn enough Spanish from a phrase book so as to make them understand his orders. As it was he was telling them what to do in English with occasional lapses into Danish, even into Faroese in moments of exasperation. They spoke a little English interlarded with many Spanish words, and this was known on the South American continent as Spangelese. The two Brazilians were pure Indians from the Amazon basin and had jet-black hair, beards, and side-whiskers. One morning I watched them at work scraping off rust—a perpetual menace—from parts of the cargo deck. The shoulder-length hair of one man was partly covered by a spotted black-and-white handkerchief. He wore a tattered khaki shirt, black jeans, long black tight boots, and a leather belt with a knife in it. The other Brazilian also had black jeans but his boots were short and his shirt green plaid. I asked about a man who took a prominent part in the Neptune ceremony on the outward voyage. He was a foreigner but I did not know what nationality. Now I learnt he originally joined the boat at Las Palmas, pilfered a warehouse when she was in dock at London so was wanted by the police there, and finally disappeared from A.E.S. at Rotterdam.

Among this crew was one Englishman who had broken his contract on a Falklands sheep farm, and was working his passage back. Another doing the same was Fred the steward, but Fred had fulfilled his contract and liked being a shepherd at North Arm so much that he wanted to renew it. He found he could not do this from Stanley but must return to England and go to the London office of the F.I.C., so now he was having doubts and had half decided he would try for agricultural work in Britain. He was very interested in my reactions to the Falklands and about the book he heard I intended to write.

Sea travel gives one a sense of distance that is lacking if one goes by air. For a couple of days we were still in radio communication with Stanley, then it ceased. As we drew nearer to the South American continent, though not near enough to see land, radio sets blared out Latin American music, gay and exciting. When darkness fell I would sit on the boat deck marvelling at the star-studded sky, picking out constellations also seen in the northern hemisphere and therefore familiar, like Orion, Cassiopeia and the Pleiades. The lovely Southern Cross was lower on the horizon each night, and soon it would vanish completely. On 24th January we passed a group of five islets known as the Abrolhas rocks, lying 30 miles opposite Bahia in Brazil and having a light on one. They are uninhabited and barren except for a few coconut palms—that, of course, we could not distinguish, but apparently on the voyage out a passenger teased Annie Bonner by pretending he could see a monkey climbing up one. Captain Svendsen said we would cross the Equator in another five days. There was no ceremony this time, and I was thankful, for Crossing The Line needs men from the Navy to make it the rollicking Neptune farce it was and always should be.

By now I had established a routine of writing, reading and lounging, broken by meals. Most of us sat on deck in the morning and the late afternoon, but stayed in our cabins to sleep during the hottest part of the day. A swing was rigged up for the two elder Peck children. The youngest was scarcely able to walk, and Kathie Jennings' baby was too young for that. On alternative evenings we had film shows, the most amusing being about a detective-cum-professor of the James Bond type and with scenes set in Denmark, or supposed to be. Captain Svendsen was doubtful about that, for one scene, said to be just outside Copenhagen, showed a hill that he said did not exist there. On non-film evenings the chief mate would tune in the radio set in the wheelhouse for me to listen to B.B.C. Overseas. Unfortunately bad reception often spoilt the programme.

Sunsets were magnificent. I was anxious to see a phenomenon called the green flash, sometimes visible as the sun's upper rim disappears below the horizon. You must have a perfectly clear horizon line, that is unbroken by hills or trees or buildings, free from cloud, and then, if you are lucky, as the sun finally vanishes you see this green blob of light. I looked again and again but without success. Often a cloud would drift across the horizon and spoil any chance. Still I did appreciate the sunsets, and I remember one where the afterglow lasted for half an hour. Fiery light peeped out behind black and golden orange, like flames on a seashore. Gradually gathering clouds stood out like grey rocks and the bits of light that filtered through grew paler and paler and paler.

This time I hardly saw any birds, though before they used to wheel round and fly over the ship in large numbers. Albatross would be busy rearing families on shore, and I suppose other species in the southern hemisphere were similarly occupied. One morning we all rushed to look at a dolphin leaping, then swimming just below the surface, with its long dark body visible in the clear sea, then again leaping up in the air. This did not please the chief mate, who said dolphins were a sign of bad weather.

On 28th January we passed within 2 miles of the archipelago of Fernando da Noronha, which comprised six islands and numerous islets and rocks. The largest, 7 miles long, is used by Brazil as a penal settlement and we were close enough to see the prison buildings, surrounding houses and a large fort. Behind were high rocky hills, really mountains, with sharp peaks. One, on an offshore islet, was so sheer and straight that it looked like the conning tower of a giant submarine. Captain Svendsen pointed out the village of Quixaba and said near it was an aerodrome. He thought the population of the islands was 2,000.

M

Two thousand, the same as on the Falklands! This brought home to me how few in numbers the Kelpers must seem when their fate is considered by the United Nations, but I think it wrong to apply a size yardstick, or a numerical one, when judging international problems. In Stanley I was shocked to hear a young B.A.S. airman say, "Why shouldn't Britain hand over the islands to Argentina? There aren't enough people to matter." In vain I argued him that the views of 2,000 should be respected just as much as those of 20 million. "And the population is going down," he went on. He was right over that because the present threat hanging over the Falklands' future has caused, and is causing, Kelpers to emigrate. Under the present immigration laws Great Britain is barred to these people of British stock who have Falkland Island passports unless an individual can prove his grandfather at least resided in Britain. This law infuriates Falkland Islanders. Many of them have settled in New Zealand, where, near Dunedin, is a large colony of them. Others are saving and hoping to join relatives and friends there. If Britain did yield to United Nations pressure, it is believed on the Falklands that Argentina would turn the islands into a penal settlement. I looked at the indented coast before my eyes, at the cliffs and sandy beaches, and I hoped that the Falkland Islands would not become to Argentina what Fernando da Noronha is to Brazil.

The temperature was 84 degrees as we approached the equator, but there was plenty of breeze so the heat did not seem oppressive, although passengers used to far lower temperatures disliked it. Our course was too far out for us to catch a glimpse of the group of solitary volcanic rocks visited by Darwin in the *Beagle* and called St. Paul's Rocks. He contrasted the high peaks of Fernando da Noronha with them just above sea level, the highest point being 50 feet. The mineralogy interested him and he wrote about their brilliant whiteness. "This is partly due to the dung of a vast multitude of seafowl, and partly to a coating of a hard glossy substance with a pearly lustre, which is intimately united to the surface of the rocks." The birds we saw were boobies and noddies and he enjoyed himself watching crabs and spiders.

We now turned north-east, heading for the Cape Verde Islands, 1,000 miles away. Meanwhile the routine of ship life continued. We passengers basked in the sun, slept, chatted, and read, while members of the crew were busy painting rails, companionways, and rigging, stopping on Saturday morning for the weekly scrub-down of decks. I began to learn more about my fellow travellers.

Sylvia Peck had spent most of her years on the Falklands on Speedwell Island, where her husband had a job. During this period her three children were born and she said how costly it was for her to come into Stanley for each birth. Because of the uncertainty of air transport due to weather conditions, the Medical Officer of Health insists on a mother staying in Stanley a whole month before the baby is due, and this has to be at her own expense, for she only goes to hospital when birth is imminent. Sylvia said that the three occasions ate up most of the savings her husband accumulated while on Camp. Originally he had been trained as an engineer and he was hoping to get a job in that line in Britain, while Sylvia wanted to use her college musical training as soon as the children were older. She showed me a few pieces she had composed and that she was wanting to market in London.

Over meals Captain Svendsen often talked about Denmark and his home there, also about voyages made to the north of Russia, to Iceland, and to Greenland. Greenland is not a productive country, yet Denmark, to whom she belongs, has built towns accommodating 5,000 people with shops and skyscraper blocks of flats. I had been to Iceland and now I wanted to see Greenland. The Shetlands were known to me, but my visits were years ago so I used to ask Kathie Jennings about present conditions. In her opinion those islands and the Falklands had much in common, but the population of the Shetlands was far greater, being more than 20,000, while Lerwick the capital had four times as many inhabitants as Stanley.

Then Richard, the photographer, used to give me vivid descriptions of his shepherding experiences in the Camp. In winter the work involved hardship, such as riding long distances to repair fences and possibly sleeping out in the cold, lying in a sleeping bag under his horse for warmth. Distance was reckoned in time taken. "I once had to relieve an isolated shepherd who radioed to say he had dreadful internal pains and thought he had appendicitis, so the manager ordered me to go and when I asked the way he said, 'You'll find it if you go straight north. It is two and a half days' ride.' " When Richard reached the shepherd, the poor man had to ride as far as the settlement. Over such country, without roads, no other transport was possible. Once he reached the settlement, the manager phoned the M.O.H., and a Beaver was sent to fetch him, this being able to come down in the harbour, whereas before the days of the little floatplanes a ship would have had to take him to Stanley. I asked if the shepherd recovered. He did, but he was suffering from something more complicated than appendicitis and had to be sent to the British hospital at Montevideo for an operation.

We passed the Cape Verde Islands by night, so missed seeing them, but we were near enough to the African west coast to have everything on deck covered with sand that was blowing from the Sahara desert, and the two Brazilians were kept busy washing the newly-painted rails, etc. We could not now expect to see land until we drew level with Madeira. Meanwhile, everyone was becoming bored with the long voyage and I noticed how conversation lagged during meals. One morning at breakfast, Richard made us all laugh by coming in and calling out, "How many shopping days to Christmas?" Someone said at the end we ought to be psychologically tested after the experience of being so long at sea. Then came the inevitable question to Captain Svendsen, who must have it constantly from passengers during the last fortnight of every voyage, "When do you think we shall be in London?" "Maybe 12th February. Maybe the 13th. Later if there is bad weather in the Bay." The Bay of Biscay! Those who were not good sailors dreaded it, but we should not enter the Bay for a good many days. First we had to pass Madeira.

Madeira came into sight, first as a dark mass, then cliffs sloping abruptly down to the sea and something that looked like a white sail but turned out to be a large waterfall. As we drew nearer, I could distinguish vineyards by the straight terraced rows of plants, and here and there was a small building, probably a hut, dotted amid the vines. No town was visible. Funchal is on the other side of the island. From the sea the land rose up to a ridge of mountains with razor-edged summits a few thousand feet high. At one point, Ponta do Pargo, was a lighthouse built on a prominence that must have been at least 1,000 feet, and Captain Svendsen drew my attention to the white tower with a house attached.

As soon as we left Madeira behind the weather worsened and our speed went down to six knots as we met an opposing wind. This continued next day and we began to abandon hope of reaching London by 13th February. The gale increased and, in spite of hating it for delaying us, I could not help enjoying the spectacle of magnificent grey-green waves breaking in fury over the bows of A.E.S. as she rode the storm. It was easy to ascend to the wheelhouse by an inside flight of stairs that led up to it from a passage outside my cabin, but from cabin to dining-room meant descending an exposed companionway, then clutching at ship rails as one struggled against wind and driving rain for a dozen yards before reaching an entrance on the lower deck. Meals were now eaten in almost monastic silence, for our minds were pre-occupied with the weather, yet we were all sick of the subject. Kathie Jennings started a sweepstake in which we guessed date and hour of arrival in London. I put 5 a.m. on Monday the 16th, but someone even more pessimistic put Tuesday the 17th. Photographer Richard was the winner for half-past seven on Sunday, and we docked just an hour earlier.

Weather improved, but it was already colder and one had to wrap up when sitting on deck. One afternoon I saw two dolphins and hoped they were not forerunners of more storms. They were, for as we entered the Bay of Biscay we encountered a truly terrifying gale. It started late one evening and only by wedging myself with suitcase and pillows in my bunk could I get any sleep. Before I did that I was wakened every five minutes by slithering up and down in my bunk. Of course cases were rolling about the cabin floor but I ignored their bumping. Next morning it was just as frightful. Roz Barnes, who was a bad sailor and preferred to remain in bed, asked me to bring her up some coffee. A.E.S. was not a luxury liner with stewards and stewardesses to wait on you. I had done this before for Roz, but today I knew I should need both hands to cling to the rails when exposed to the elements so promised to ask Fred to bring her some. He did eventually, but not at first, for when I got down I found the passageway slippery with water and most of the passengers in the lounge looking worried and scared.

One of the Sørensen ships had gone down in the Bay, but all

her crew were safe. Our captain had a radio message to go to the assistance of a sinking Belgian vessel some 70 miles southwest, so we had turned around and were heading back south, but he had not yet been able to ascertain her exact position. Crashes from the galley showed that attempts were being made to provide us with breakfast but as yet there was no sign of it in the dining-room. The two elder little Peck girls sat together in an armchair obeying their mother's instructions not to move. The youngest of the Pecks, still a baby, grizzled mournfully but not loudly. She was obviously hungry and simply could not understand why her mother made no attempt to get her something to eat.

We sat in a stupor until we were suddenly aroused by a different noise, that of a crash made by someone falling in the passage. It was Mrs. Jennings senior, who had skidded on the slippery wet floor. No bones appeared to be broken but her face was bruised and streaming blood, and she was very badly shaken. Two of the men got her into a chair. Someone got water. Someone else mopped her face. Word quickly travelled to the wheelhouse, for Captain Svendsen and the chief mate came in turn to see if she was seriously hurt. Fortunately she was not, and coffee now provided by Fred helped her to feel better. There was no sit-down breakfast that morning. Pots of coffee, hunks of bread, slabs of butter and cheese were set on a rail-enclosed side table, and with great difficulty we kept our balance as we poured coffee and spread butter and cheese on bread. The Peck baby's lamentations changed to gurgles of delight when her mother gave her a piece of buttered bread. The only other happy creature was the Quigley poodle, who trotted gaily round, not minding the tossing of the ship or the gale outside. The ironical thing was that now the sun was shining brilliantly, the rain having stopped; but the wind was blowing just as hard and the waves were still colossally high and violent. Spray was drenching the part along which I had to walk to get to the companionway, and I had to wait for a second between waves to avoid being soaked.

Upstairs I found Roz was very alarmed. Fred had taken her coffee and after drinking it she had gone to the wheelhouse. She said the situation was very bad indeed, and she had been in many storms with Sid in his sea-captain days. She heard that another ship had reached the Belgian vessel so we had turned round again to head north, but we were making no progress, being driven backwards if anything. Apparently we were trying to go north-west, somewhat off normal course but in an endeavour to avoid being driven nearer the French coast, where the gale was at its height. Roz insisted on getting out the life jackets and putting clothes and vital documents and money ready, just in case of an immediate call for passengers to go to the boat stations. It was terrifying, though one could not do anything but wait passively for one was helpless against the elements. I spent the rest of the morning lying wedged in my bunk. It was the most comfortable place to be in. Reading was impossible with the pitching and tossing so I closed my eyes and tried to picture a serene wood in summer, a wood far away from the sea.

Captain Svendsen joined us at dinner to my great relief, for the crisis could not be too bad or he would not have left the bridge. He said that the Sørensen Company ship wrecked was 700 tons and going from Cornwall to Algeciras with china clay, and that captain and crew were taken off by a German boat. Thankfully eating pork chops, potatoes and tinned fruit, with rails fixed to the table to keep food from sliding off—but even so it was difficult not to lose half—we all restrained ourselves from asking Captain Svendsen futile questions about our position and when we should reach London. I could read the thoughts of the others and knew mine were running along the same lines. We were really like anxious relations of a patient on whom a surgeon had just performed a complicated operation and we knew it was useless to enquire whether this was a success or not. Mrs. Jennings senior was at dinner, pluckily declaring she felt all right, though her mouth, cheek and one eye were black with bruises.

The sea was not so violent that evening. We were on course and it was steady enough to play bingo. The chief mate said we were doing 6 knots when he appeared in the doorway to tell us clocks were being moved forward one hour that night, the third time during the voyage. We should then be using Greenwich Mean Time. Richard teased me by explaining that was because we had been nearly driven back as far as Madeira, and for a moment I was foolish enough to believe him.

We entered the English Channel on Friday, 13th February,

and were getting along splendidly until a vile easterly wind blew up. Then we ran into dense fog. The ship's hooter was going continually and its miserable warning sound made me very depressed. Also I was cold, for the radiator in the cabin was not working properly. Captain Svendsen promised to have it seen to and meanwhile lent me his own electric fire. I finished reading my fourteenth book on this voyage and tried out a new patience game called Crossword that Kathie Jennings showed me. Later the sun broke through the fog and at supper Captain Svendsen spoke hopefully of our docking late Sunday night. Clocks went on another hour to British Standard Time. We were really getting home at last.

On the thirty-first day at sea, I came down to breakfast to see a rope ladder in readiness for a pilot. It was foggy again, but by half-past nine I could see Folkestone, and how lovely the buildings and trees looked! Never had I imagined I should be so thrilled to see the white cliffs of Kent again.

We slowed to a crawl. The 'pilot wanted' flag was flying and the chief mate stood waiting by the rope ladder. Then I saw a Trinity House launch approach, pilot climb aboard, be greeted by mate, and escorted up a companionway to the wheelhouse. While we were having mid-morning coffee, Captain Svendsen came in offering a Sunday newspaper brought by the pilot. I was the first to get it and spent the rest of the morning gloating over this first up-to-date newspaper that I had seen for twenty-three weeks. I read everything in it—strikes, weather, book reviews, sports events, fashions, slimming diets, even advertisements. There was actually an item of news about the Falklands, described as islands "in the South Atlantic, off the coast of South America". A Mr. Hill, "retired builder and amateur naturalist" had just bought two of them, Grand Jason and Steeple Jason, in order to study penguins, albatross, and "some rare hawks". The new owner was reported as saying he intended to visit them once a year and that he thought of chartering a plane from Montevideo to fly out to them. This naïve disposal of travel difficulties amused all the passengers. The Jasons are a group of small islands north of Carcass Island, and the two purchased are the farthest out. They cannot possibly have landing ground for an aeroplane while they look on the map too exposed for a Beaver floatplane. Uninhabited, they used to be farmed by the manager of Pebble Island, who made the 60-mile journey by sea.

It was a lovely sunny afternoon and there were ships everywhere. A.E.S. seamen were loosening the derricks, removing ropes that lashed several huge packing cases, and when we passed Tilbury at half-past five I could see the gangway was in readiness. We still had to go up the Thames as far as the West India Dock. The sun was sinking, the water grey, and on either side were ugly grey industrial buildings, but I was supremely happy, and the sight of a London bus as exciting as that of a few stunted trees.

Not until nine o'clock did I get into a taxi to be driven to a London hotel. It was a long way from the docks but I did not mind for it enthralled me to see familiar landmarks like St. Paul's, such a colossus when compared with Stanley's Christ Church, the most southerly and I should think the smallest cathedral in existence. After reaching my hotel, I soon sought the restaurant to enjoy the type of food I had been denied so long—fresh salad and fresh fruit.

Facing London street traffic next morning I expected to feel scared, but strangely enough I might never have been away. What did strike me as new? First was the sight of one woman in every four wearing a maxi-coat, a fashion not launched when I left England the summer before. Secondly I missed the ten-shilling note. It was difficult to distinguish the substitute coin of fifty new pence until I got accustomed to its bevelled edges and could pick it out from other values in my purse. That first morning after arrival in London, I went to a hairdresser, I gazed and gazed at shop windows, I had lunch at a busy restaurant, and after that I walked in Hyde Park, looking at the great trees and wondering how I had existed so long without them.

Yes, on the Falklands I missed many things to which I was accustomed, but I shall always be thankful that I have seen these far-away unique islands. Already time is blurring the memory of what I did not like—the searing winds, the lack of so much, and the oppressive isolation—and instead I dwell, almost nostalgically, on the beauty of the harbours, of tussac-covered islands, of gorse hedges and diddle dee, of penguins and sea lions and those amazing rivers of stone. Whether or not I ever re-visit the Falkland Islands, they have become an integral part of me.

Chronological List of Dates

1592   Discovery by Captain John Davis in ship *Desire*. Called at first Davis' Southern Islands.

1690   Landing made by Captain John Strong. He named the passage between the two large east and west islands Falkland Sound, in honour of Anthony Cary, fifth Viscount Falkland and then Treasurer of the Navy. Later the whole group of islands was called the Falklands.

1701   Landing by French.

1716   French named the islands Iles Malouines.

1764   French established a settlement and called it Port Louis.

1765   Ignorant of French settlement, the British Government sent Commodore John Byron to survey the islands. He landed on Saunders Island, set up Port Egmont settlement there, and claimed the entire group for Britain.

1766   France ceded the Iles Malouines to Spain. Spain renamed Port Louis, calling it Port Soledad.

1774   Due to economic difficulties in Britain, Port Egmont was evacuated, but the garrison left behind an inscription stating that the Falkland Islands belonged to the King of Great Britain.

1810   Separation of South American colonies from Spain. Spanish governor at Port Soledad fled to Montevideo on the mainland.

1816   The newly-formed United Provinces of Rio de la Plata claimed islands.

1820   Government of the United Provinces formally took possession.

1831   As a reprisal for seizing an American sealer, Port Soledad was sacked by the American (United States) corvette *Lexington* and the chief settlers carried away as prisoners.

1833   Britain returned to the Falklands and claimed them as her possession. She began to colonize them.

1851   Formation of Falkland Islands Trading Company.

1892   The Falklands created a Crown Colony.

1964   'Token invasion' by Condor Group from Argentina.

1968   Lord Chalfont's mission to the Falklands concerning their future.

Selected Bibliography

Boyson, V. F., *The Falkland Islands*, Clarendon Press (Oxford, 1924).
Cawkell, M. B. R. and others, *The Falkland Islands*, Macmillan (London, 1960).
Cobb, A. E., *Birds of the Falkland Islands*, Witherby (London, 1933).
Commonwealth Office, *Biennial report on Falkland Islands and Dependencies*, H.M.S.O. (London, 1969).
Falkland Islands Co. Ltd., *The Falkland Islands Company Ltd., 1851–1951*, privately printed (London, 1951).
Falkland Islands Periodicals (printed in Stanley):
   Journal, 1967, 1968, 1969–
   Magazine, 1889–1927.
   Monthly Review, 1958–
Gift, Theo, *An Island Princess*, Lawrence & Bullen (London, 1893). Fiction.
Gorbell jnr, Julius, *Struggle for the Falkland Islands*, Oxford University Press (London, 1927).
Grant, B. S. H., *Postage stamps of the Falkland Islands and Dependencies*, Stanley Gibbons Ltd. (London, 1952).
Hickling, Harold, *Sailor at Sea*, William Kimber (London, 1965). Has chapters dealing with Falklands during World War I.
McKinnon, L. B., *Some Account of the Falkland Islands*, privately printed (London, 1840).
McWhan, W. F., *The Falkland Islands Today*, Tract Enterprise (Stirling, 1952).
Metford, John, "Falklands or Malvinas? The background to the dispute." (In *International Affairs*, Vol. 44, No. 3, 1968).
Millam, Peter J., *Centenary of the consecration of Waite Hockin Stirling as first bishop of the Falkland Islands*, Government Printing Press (Stanley, 1969). Souvenir booklet.
O'Brien, Conor, "From the Outposts: the Falkland Islands" (In *Blackwood's Magazine*, Vol. 218, 1925).
Pettingill, Eleanor, *Penguin Summer*, Cassell (London, 1962).
Potter, John Deane, *No Time for Breakfast*, Andrew Melrose (London, 1951). Pages 213–25 deal with the Falklands.
Smith, John, *Condemned at Stanley: notes and sketches on the hulks and wrecks at Port Stanley*, privately printed (Stanley, 1969).

Stirling, Waite Hockin, Bishop of Falkland Islands, *The Falkland Islands and Tierra del Fuego*, privately printed (Buenos Aires, 1891). Reprinted at Stanley, 1969.

Vallentin, E. F., *Illustrations of the Flowering Plants and Ferns of the Falkland Islands*, Reeve (London, 1921).

Whittington, G. T., *The Falkland Islands*, privately printed (London, 1840).

Some VOYAGES that include visits to the Falkland Islands:

Anson, George, *Voyage round the World in the Years 1740–44*.

Bone, David W., *The Brassbounder*, 1910.

Coppinger, R. W., *Cruise of the Alert in 1878–82*.

Darwin, Charles, *Voyage of the Beagle, 1833–38*.

Murdoch, W. G. B., *From Edinburgh to the Antarctic*, 1894.

Snow, Parker, *Voyage to the South Seas and Tierra del Fuego*, 1857.

Spry, W. J. J., *Cruise of the Challenger*, 1876.

Index

Pensions, 134
Periodicals: *Falkland Islands Journal*, 113, 146; *Falkland Islands Magazine*, 113, 133; *Falkland Islands Monthly Review*, 93, 98, 113, 114, 116, 142, 161, 166
Police, 128
Population, 10, 14, 21, 129, 178
Port Egmont, 14, 147; *see also* Saunders Island
Port Howard, 68, 76, 156–7
Port Louis, 14, 42, 149–50, 153
Port San Carlos, 69, 153, 156
Port Stephens, 45, 70–71, 76, 104–5, 140
Port William, 39, 88
Postage stamps, 92–3
Postal service, 21, 119
Printing works, 137–8
Punta Arenas, 11, 162

Q

Quarks, 62, 106, 141, 146
Quartz rocks, 23, 39, 81

R

Radio, 52–3, 129
Radio telephone, 19, 52, 80, 84, 88, 156, 159
Rincon Grande, 152
Roads, absence of, 21–2
Roy Cove, 143, 144–5
Royalty, Visits from, 112–13

S

Salvador, 118, 152–3
San Carlos, 15, 153–5
Saunders Island, 14, 66, 67, 147; *see also*, Port Egmont
Sea elephants, *see* Elephant seals
Sea lions, 70, 105–6, 110
Sea Lions Island, 70, 84
Seaweed, *see* Kelp
Sedge Island, 83
Sheep farming, 21, 22, 77–8, 100, 102, 136, 137, 140, 144

Shepherdesses, 95, 100–101
Social clubs, 59–60
South Georgia, 53, 149, 161
Sparrow Cove, 40, 170
Speedwell Island, 70, 140, 179
Split Island, 83
Staats Island, 66, 83
Stanley: arrival, 43–5; Battle Memorial, 112; cathedral, 42, 89, 92, 113; description, 42–3, 46–7, 50–61; history, 42–3; Ship Hotel, 27; shops, 47–8, 87; Town Council, 125–8; Upland Goose Hotel, 119, 167; Whalebone Arch, 112
Stirling, Bishop: centenary of consecration, 92–3
Stone runs, 39–40, 75, 143
Strong, Captain, 9
Surf Bay, 61–2

T

Teal Inlet, 152
Telephone, 54
Terriss, Ellaline, 27
Trees, 23, 46, 79, 141, 145, 146, 147, 160
Trieste Island, 62, 105–6
Troupials, red-breasted, 60
Tussac birds, 110
Tussac grass, 83, 84, 105, 108–9, 142
Twins, The, 70, 146

V

Volunteer Point, 149

W

Weddell Island, 62, 64–83, 140–41
West Point Island, 24, 145, 146
Wild life conservation, 24
Wool, 20, 22, 79, 136, 140, 145, 151, 168
Wrecks, 91; *see also*, *Charles Cooper*, *Great Britain*